A Man's Place is in the Kitchen

Published by   Grendel Press
               P.O. Box 238
               Loveland, CO 80539
First Edition

For information about products from Grendel Press,
please call toll-free 1-866-GRENDEL or visit www.grendelpress.com

ISBN: 0-9714988-2-2
Library of Congress Control Number: 2002100513

Photographer: Kate Porter
Editor: Mary Boone
Cover design by Erik Watada

Do I Hear the Dinner Bell?

I will never be a good cook. I can wreck a kitchen trying to make tea. Also, it takes a special kind of flair I don't have. I cannot bring myself to fling a chicken across the sink like Julia Child. Nor can I prance among the pots like Graham Kerr with all those pearly teeth showing. Asking me to cook a dinner is like asking Larry, Curley and Moe to play a Mozart trio—a very "iffy" proposition at best.

I fear I am destined to remain what I have always been: not a food critic, but a walking, rampant appetite. I am a one-man cheering section for chefs of every size and stripe—of every accent and style. As a result, I get invited to dinner a heck of a lot more often than most other civilians!

But, I didn't horn into this book for no good reason. Because of my fame as a "gran appetite," Chef Scott has paid me $12 million to say some clever things about his new cookbook, *A Man's Place is in the Kitchen*. I would have taken the job for free, but don't tell him that; he's rich and can afford all the bragging I'm about to do.

Seriously folks, Scott can cut it.

Back in the days before I got rich myself, I used to show up at his door looking starved as often as I could get away with it. The reason? Nothing pleases this Sultan of the Saucepan more than hearing all those wild praises around his table from fans, old and new.

So, if you want to learn all sorts of culinary secrets and become a social success like Scott Avery, then lay hands on his book. But, for god's sake, pay for it—I haven't collected my big fee yet!

Gary Travis
CEO Cybrgold Cos.

ABOUT THE AUTHOR

Scott Avery, a self-styled kitchen guru, entered the world in a taxi attempting to negotiate the slopes of a sleepy New England town during the early morning hours of the worst blizzard of 1935. Needless to say, he was cold and hungry. Hospital food being what it sometimes can be, he quickly developed an interest in good vittles; that attraction remains with him to this day.

But alas, food didn't become Scott's major concern for quite a few years. First came stints as a DJ, radio and TV announcer, and actor. As you may imagine, those careers brought with them some "lean" years, during which the food business came into play. Loving the idea of being able to eat, he became active in the restaurant business while waiting for his big break.

It started with washing dishes, bussing tables, then waiting on table and, finally, restaurant management. He eventually began work with Marriott Hotels, where he accepted a position as an assistant restaurant manager. He rapidly moved to the position of restaurant manager, catering service manager, catering sales manager, and then director of catering at the world-famous Marriott Santa Barbara Biltmore. From there, he became vice president and chef, in partnership with longtime friends in their own Santa Barbara dinner-theatre, the Le P'tit Cabaret. (Please note he also received critical reviews as an actor in such productions as *The Sunshine Boys* and *Same Time Next Year.*)

In addition to his love of food, Scott developed an interest in flowers and their ability to enhance the presentation of food. Self-taught, he rose to become a partner in a large floral design studio, The Sherwood Forest in Burbank, Calif. He became one of the top designers in southern California, with his designs being seen in many memorable films, and virtually every television series of the time, including *Fantasy Island, Mommie Dearest, Code Red, Gloria* and *One Day at a Time.*

Proving that a person who applies himself can do just about any and every thing well, he presents this, his first epistle.

Dedication

Dedicated to those countless friends, relatives and acquaintances who, over the years, have graciously shared their recipes and secrets (culinary and otherwise) with me and, hence, with all of you.

"Man's mind stretched to a new idea never goes back to its original dimensions."
—Oliver Wendell Holmes

PROLOGUE

At the risk of committing heresy, I have attempted to show in the following pages that *A Man's Place is in the Kitchen*—not just propped over the barbeque pit or opening a can of soup, but actually in the kitchen preparing real food.

Although it's common knowledge that many of the world's greatest chefs are men, cooking at home still seems to be shrouded in mystery and myth: "Men aren't SUPPOSED to cook." The stereotypical roles for men and women are changing. In an economy where Mom also often works or is off flying fighter jets or driving tanks, there's an expanding awareness and sharing of household obligations. Today, you may find Mom taking out the trash, fixing the faucet and running to the office, while Dad spends his time changing diapers, making beds and (of ALL things) cooking. And, very often, you'll find men who believe cooking can be fun and isn't all that difficult.

Men who haven't tried cooking may find they like it…if they can just get past their fears. That's right…ANYONE can cook and ENJOY it! The by-word is FUN! As you enter this wonderful new world of endless creativity, you'll find ideas and recipes from all over the planet with which I encourage you to experiment.

So, now's the time: Let's explore the myths, banish the fears and confidently enter that Inner Sanctum known as "The Kitchen." You'll have fun preparing tempting, nutritionally balanced meals that will earn you praise from everyone.

So men, be receptive to new ideas and enjoy the creative opportunities ahead. Oh, by the way, all you ladies—Sis, Grandma (and yes, even you, Mom) are invited to come along as we dare to enter a new frontier.

Good luck and much fun for you all!

—Scott Avery

ABOUT THE BOOK

A*Man's Place is in the Kitchen* isn't meant to be a "be all, end all" of the cooking arena, but rather a humorous and, at times, irreverent compilation of advice and anecdotes. It includes the "Who, What, Where, When, Why and How" of cooking, along with some "crown jewels of the kitchen," memorable quotes and recipes collected from all over the world.

The book is designed to encourage everyone—male and female—with the basic premise that ANYONE can cook, if they have the proper guidance and if they find the fun in it. *A Man's Place* will steer the uninitiated through the perilous culinary jungle.

All thoughts, suggestions, interpretations, ideas and implications contained herein are those of the writer and other quotable sources. The book was drafted with healthy individuals in mind. Those with special dietary requirements or health problems, or anyone having any questions about any suggestions made on these pages, should consult their physician, dietician, or healthcare professional. The book is presented for educational and entertainment purposes only

A Man's Place includes recipes I've created along with those I've compiled and collected on my travels to French farmhouses, Italian villas, local inns, and the kitchens of friends and relatives. They're simple to follow and may provide an alternative to frozen and microwave-ready meals. The recipes are delicious, fairly quick to prepare and maybe, just maybe, they'll take years off your waistline. So, take a peek inside these covers to see (where you think) no man has dared go before.

"The world is a book, and those
that do not travel read only one page."
—St. Augustine

Table of Contents

IN THE BEGINNING:
what you'll need to know

"Energy and persistence conquer all things."
—Benjamin Franklin

While you could go crazy (and broke) trying to figure out and purchase ALL the items on the market for every type of kitchen—including the "professional" and "gourmet"—my suggestion is: keep it basic and simple. As you progress in your abilities and creativity, you can add to your "Batterie de Cuisine."

COMING TO TERMS

If you've never had to confront them, cooking terms can be intimidating and downright frustrating. But, if you'll take a little time, and keep this information handy for reference, you'll quickly adjust to these new terms. Here are some of the more common; others may be explained as they occur.

COMMON COOKING TERMS

TERM	MEANING
Au jus	In its own juices (usually beef juices)
Al dente *(No, not the barber.)*	Italian for "tender but firm"
A la	In the style of
Amandine	Made or served with almonds
Bake	Cook by dry oven heat
Baste	Brush or spoon liquids or drippings over food during cooking; prevents drying
Batter	A mixture of uncooked eggs, flour and liquid
Batterie de cuisine	All the items needed for cooking
Beat	Mix very briskly with a whip, spoon or beater
Beurre	French for butter
Bind *(No, not tied up.)*	Stir an ingredient into any mixture to help hold it together
Bisque	A creamed soup
Blend	Mix ingredients together until smooth
Blanch *(No, not DuBois.)*	Briefly immerse in boiling water
Boeuf	French for beef
Boil	Cook items in boiling water
Braise or Sauté	Brown in fat; cook uncovered on range
Bread *(No, not a sandwich.)*	Coat an item with breadcrumbs
Brush	Apply liquids with a basting brush
Café	French for coffee
Candy *(No M&Ms please.)*	Glaze with syrup
Chill	Refrigerate until cold
Chop	Cut into small pieces or cubes
Coat	Dip in egg wash, flour and breadcrumbs
Crème	French for cream
Deglaze	With a bit of liquid, scraping browned meat bits from the bottom of an oven pan or skillet
Dice	Cut into very small bits
Dilute	Thin with water or other liquid
Dredge	Coat with flour or other dry ingredient
Drizzle	A very fine pouring of liquid over solid foods
Dust	Lightly coat an item – usually with confectioners' sugar or flour
En brochette	A variety of foods cooked on a skewer
Entree	The main course
Filet	Boneless fish or meat

Flour *(Nope, NOT a daisy.)*	Coating food with flour
Fold	Mix and blend gently with an overhand motion
Freeze	Chill until frozen
Grate	To fragment or shred foods using a grater
Grill	Broil on a grill
Julienne	Cut into narrow strips (usually vegetables)
Marinate	To soak a food in spiced liquids
Mash	Reduce to a pulp
Melt	Liquefy by heating
Mince	Cut into extremely fine pieces
Mix	Stir and blend together
Mocha	A combination of chocolate and coffee
Peel	To pare or cut away skin of fruit or vegetables
Pinch	An amount less than 1/8 teaspoon
Pit	Remove pits—usually from avocados/peaches
Poach	Simmer in liquid
Poulet	French for chicken
Preheat	Bring to required temperature before use
Puree	Turn into a paste form in a blender
Ramekin	A single-serving baking dish
Roast	Oven cook by dry heat
Sauté	Pan fry
Scald	Heat milk or cream just to the boiling point
Season *(No, not summer.)*	Add seasonings such as salt and pepper
Seed	Remove seeds from fruits or vegetables
Shred	Cut into thin strips using a grater or tear into shreds by hand
Shuck	Remove shells from shellfish or husks from corn
Sift	Pass dry ingredients through a strainer
Simmer	Cook over very low heat
Skim	Remove fat surface from liquids like soups
Steam *(Don't get angry.)*	Cook by steaming
Stew	Cook completely covered with water. Also, a type of soup
Stir	To mix or blend using a circular motion
Stir-fry	Cook quickly, constantly stirring and tossing
Stuff	The act of stuffing, as a chicken or turkey
Syrupy	The consistency of syrup
Tenderize	Make tender, using a mallet, tenderizer or marinade
Thicken	Thicken a liquid, usually with flour or cornstarch
Thin	To dilute with a liquid
Toss	To mix or combine ingredients, as in a salad
Whip *(No! No! No!)*	Beat until stiff with a wire whip or beater
Whisk	A utensil of looped wire for whipping
Zest	The scraped rind of various citrus fruits

THE BASICS

With most of these items handy, you should be able to accomplish your basic cooking goals.

SKILLETS, PANS, KETTLES: all with covers. Teflon-coated is the best and often least expensive. Copper is elegant and excellent, but expensive (and miserable to clean).

1 – 6-inch skillet	1 – 10-inch skillet	1 – 12-inch skillet
1 – 10-inch iron skillet	1 – 2-quart Dutch oven	1 – 1- or 2-gallon kettle
1 – steamer pan	1 – steamer basket	1 – deep fryer
1 – stock pot	1 – set of saucepans (1-, 2- and 3-quart sizes)	

CUTLERY

1 – slicing knife	1 – paring knife	1 – carving set
1 – chopping knife	1 – vegetable peeler	1 – apple corer
1 – bread knife	1 – large cutting board	

APPLIANCES

1 – electric blender	1 – hand-held electric mixer
1 – electric carving knife	

OVEN & DISHWARE

6 – ramekins or soufflé cups	1 – 1 1/2 -quart covered casserole
1 – 2-quart covered casserole	1 – 3-quart covered casserole
1 – set of standard mixing bowls	2 – 8-cup muffin pans
1 – cookie sheet	1 – 3-by-5-by-9-inch loaf pan
1 – 2-by-9-by-13-inch loaf pan	1 – 8-inch square cake pan
2 – 9-inch round cake pans	2 – 9-inch pie pans
1 – large covered roaster with rack	

KITCHEN UTENSILS

1 – set liquid measuring cups	1 – dry measuring nest
1 – set measuring spoons	1 – set funnels
1 – small wire whisk	1 – large wire whisk
1 – potato masher	1 – baster
1 – set large tongs	1 – soup ladle
1 – long-handled cooking fork	2 – long-handled cooking spoons
1 – long-handled slotted spoon	1 – set wooden spoons
1 – grater	1 – strainer
1 – set spatulas, large and small	1 – set rubber spatulas
1 – flour sifter	1 – rolling pin
1 – cake rack	1 – wooden mallet
2 – pastry brushes	1 – vegetable brush
1 – meat thermometer	1 – candy/fat thermometer
1 – oven thermometer	1 – set oven mitts
1 – set pot holders	1 – timer (may already be on your stove or microwave)

Too Much Too Soon - Too Little Too Late

Unless you have that sixth sense (or until you develop it), stay out of trouble by following the recipes. Here is a common list of measures, weights and temperatures and some tips you'll want to keep handy.

TIPS FOR MEASURING

1. When measuring brown sugar, always make sure it is firmly packed.
2. Sift dry ingredients before measuring.
3. Measure liquids while cup is level; check quantity at eye level.
4. When using measuring spoons or cups, level off ingredients with the flat side of a knife.

MEASUREMENT EQUIVALENCES

Pinch or dash . . . . 1/8 teaspoon or less	**1 cup** . . . . .16 tablespoons (8 fluid ounces)
1 teaspoon . . . . 5 grams	**1 pint** . . . . 2 cups (16 fluid ounces)
1 tablespoon . . . . 3 teaspoons	**1 quart** . . . . 2 pints (32 fluid ounces)
1 fluid ounce . . . . 2 tablespoons	**1 gallon** . . . . 4 quarts (128 fluid ounces)
1/4 cup . . . . . . .4 tablespoons / 2 fluid ounces	**2 gallons** . . . . 1 peck
1/3 cup . . . . 5 tablespoons +	**4 pecks** . . . . 1 bushel
1 teaspoon (2 2/3 fluid ounces)	**1 ounce** . . . . 28.35 grams
1/2 cup . . . . 8 tablespoons (4 fluid ounces)	**1 pound** . . . . 16 ounces

MEASURES IN METRIC CONVERSIONS

1 ounce . . . . 28.35 grams
454 grams . . . . 1 pound
2.2 pounds . . . . 1 kilogram
1 teaspoon . . . . 5 milliliters
1 tablespoon . . . . 15 milliliters
1 cup . . . . .24 liters (250 milliliters)
1 gallon . . . . 3.8 liters

WEIGHT OF COMMON INGREDIENTS

FOOD	WEIGHT OF 1 CUP
Sifted all-purpose flour	. . . . . . .5 ounces
Butter or solid shortening	. . . . .8 ounces
Sifted cake flour	. . . . .3 1/2 ounces
Grated cheese	. . . . .4 ounces
Whole eggs	. . . . .8 ounces
Honey	. . . . 12 ounces
Milk	. . . . .8 ounces
Coarsely chopped nuts	. . . . . . .4 ounces
Granulated sugar	. . . . .7 ounces
Packed brown sugar	. . . . . .7 1/2 ounces
Powdered sugar	. . . . .4 ounces
Vegetable oil	. . . . .9 ounces

HOW MUCH IS...?

1 pound apples	. . . . About 4 medium
1 pound bananas	. . . . . . About 4 medium
1 pound raisins	. . . . About 3 cups
1 pound oranges	. . . . . . About 3 medium
1 pound mushrooms	.About 6 cups sliced
1 pound potatoes	. . . . . . About 3 medium
1 pound butter	. . . . About 2 cups
1 pound milk	. . . . .About 4 cups
1 pound spaghetti	. About 7 cups cooked
1 pound rice	. . . . . . About 7 cups cooked
1 pound salt	. . . . About 2 cups
1 pound sugar	. . . . About 2 cups
1 pound coffee	About 3 1/2 cups ground

TEMPERATURES

F = Fahrenheit   C = Celsius   ° = degrees

Freezing point of water	32° F (0° C)
Simmering point of water	180° F(82° C)
Boiling point of water	212° F (100° C)
Soft ball stage for sugar syrup	240° F (116° C)
Hard ball stage for sugar syrup	265° F (127° C)
Hard crack stage for sugar syrup	300° F(149° C)
Sugar caramelizes	338° F (170° C)
Very low oven	Under 300° F (148.8° C)
Low oven	325° to 350° F (162.7° to 176.6° C)
Moderate oven	350° to 375° F (176.6° to 190.5° C)
Hot oven	400° to 425° F (204.4° to 218.3° C)
Very hot oven	Over 450° F (232.2° C)

EMERGENCY SUBSTITUTIONS

IF YOU NEED:	YOU CAN USE IN A PINCH:
1 cup cake flour	1 cup minus 2 tablespoons all-purpose flour
1 tablespoon cornstarch	2 tablespoons all-purpose flour
1 teaspoon baking powder	1/2 teaspoon cream of tartar plus 1/4 teaspoon baking soda
1 package active dry yeast	1 cake compressed yeast or 2 1/4 teaspoons yeast
1 cup granulated sugar	1 cup packed brown sugar or 2 cups powdered sugar
1 cup corn syrup	1 cup sugar plus 1/4 cup water
1 ounce (1 square) unsweetened chocolate	3 tablespoons unsweetened cocoa powder plus 1 tablespoon shortening or cooking oil
1 cup buttermilk	1 cup plain yogurt or 1 tablespoon lemon juice or vinegar plus enough whole milk to make 1 cup (let stand 5 minutes before using.) Or 1 cup whole milk plus 1 3/4 teaspoons cream of tarter
1 cup light cream	1 tablespoon melted butter plus enough whole milk to make 1 cup

Health Points to Ponder

Some of these foods may still be safely consumed beyond these times, but we err on the side of discretion and feel these foods should NOT be consumed beyond the "Use By" dates. Always read the labels for these dates.

MAXIMUM STORAGE TIME - REFRIGERATED FOODS	
Refrigerated food	Maximum Storage Time
Fresh poultry products	3 days
Leftover cooked poultry (turkey, stuffing, etc.)	2 days
Fresh live lobster (packed in seaweed)	6 to 7 hours
Fresh fish	2 days
Shellfish	1 day
Leftover fish and cooked shellfish	2 days
Raw, fresh vegetables (broccoli, beans, asparagus, etc.)	4 days
Raw root vegetables (carrots, turnips, etc.)	14 days
Raw leaf vegetables (celery, cabbage, etc.)	7 days
Raw corn (on the cob with husks)	1 day
Raw squash varieties, cucumbers, etc.	7 days
Leafy salad greens, mushrooms, potatoes, etc.	7 days
Cooked leftover veggies	2 days
Whole raw eggs (stored in carton)	8 to 10 days
Hard boiled eggs (in shell)	10 days
Butter and margarine (wrapped)	14 days
Fresh milk, cream	4 to 6 days
Processed cheeses	14 days
Hard cheeses	6 to 10 months
Fruit juices	7 days
Fresh fruits	1 to 2 weeks
Cooked fruits	7 days
Uncooked meats (steaks, chops, roasts, etc.)	5 days
Uncooked meats (ground and varietal)	2 days
Cured meats (bacon, ham, lunchmeats, hot dogs, etc.)	3 to 5 days
Mayonnaise	2 months
Peanut butter	2 to 3 months
Pickles	2 months
Mustard	8 months
Catsup and olives	2 months
Salad dressings	3 months
Baby food	2 days
Jams and jellies	1 year

MAXIMUM STORAGE TIME - FROZEN FOODS

Refrigerated food	Max. Storage Time
Vegetables	1 year
Butter and margarine	1 year
Eggs (yolks and whites separately)	1 year
Baked breads and rolls	6 to 8 months
Baked pies	6 to 8 months
Baked cakes and cookies	6 to 8 months
Ground meat	3 months
Fresh raw meats (beef, lamb)	1 year
Cooked meats	4 to 6 months
Fresh pork	6 months
Fresh livers, hearts, etc.	3 months
Fresh poultry (chicken, turkey)	6 to 12 months
Cooked poultry	4 to 6 months
Fresh seafood and shellfish	4 months
Cooked seafood and shellfish	2 months

MAXIMUM SHELF TIME – PANTRY ITEMS

Food	Max. Storage Time
Canned foods in general	2 to 3 years
Sugars (tightly stored)	6 months
Oils	1 year
Preserves, condiments, jellies	1 year
Starches, baking sodas and powders	6 months
Pastas	6 months
Rice	Ad infinitum
Syrups	Ad infinitum
Cereals	3 months
Dried foods	1 year
Freeze-dried foods	Ad infinitum
Dehydrated foods	6 months
Salad dressings	6 months

OTHER SAFETY CONSIDERATIONS

- If a can is bulging, do NOT use it. The food has spoiled.
- Do NOT use packages of food that have been torn or ripped open.
- Be sure to ROTATE stored foods, using the oldest first; this includes fresh, frozen and packaged.
- Date ALL food packages so rotation is accurate.
- Try to use foods BEFORE their maximum storage time is up.
- Clean your refrigerator regularly.
- When storing frozen foods, do NOT rinse prior to wrapping.
- DO remove fresh meats and fish from store wrappings, and rewrap before freezing or refrigerating.
- If there is a power failure, leave doors to freezer and refrigerator CLOSED; foods will keep well for several hours.
- When handling fresh, uncooked meats or seafood of any kind, be sure to wash your hands frequently, and before touching any other foods to avoid cross-contamination. Surfaces that have come in contact with one food item MUST be sanitized before coming in contact with any other. All utensils used in contact with one item, MUST be sanitized before using with any other. NEVER use the same plate for uncooked and then cooked foods.
- Remember to avoid what is called DOUBLE DIPPING, or using one utensil to prepare more than one item, such as knives, scoops, spoons, etc., in items such as mayonnaise, mustard, etc.
- Be sure to keep hot foods hot (about 140 internal degrees) and cold foods cold (about 40 degrees). Buffet items should be left out no longer than two hours (or if it's REALLY hot, one hour). Leftover foods should be refrigerated AS SOON AS POSSIBLE to avoid contamination. If it's been sitting out more than 2 hours, discard it.
- If you stuff a chicken or turkey, remove the stuffing and wrap it separately before refrigerating.
- When cooking, remember that actual cooking times may vary from the recipe, due to individual cooking styles, personal interpretations of amounts of flame, and the fact that ovens vary in calibration.
- A good rule of thumb is "when in doubt, throw it out!" We tend to think if something is refrigerated, it'll last forever, which is a great way to get ill.

According to the U.S. Department of Agriculture, we must pay special attention to several important things, so we list them here for your undivided consideration:
- Know the difference between "Use By" and "Sell By" dates. To be safe, do NOT buy or use after the "Use By" date.
- Set your refrigerator temperature at 35 to 40 degrees.
- Do NOT risk cross-contamination from bacteria by "double-dipping." Use clean utensils for each item, EVERY time.
- Under NO circumstances, should raw poultry – or ANY meats or seafood-be left standing at room temperature for ANY length of time.

THE *MAGIC* OF HERBS & SPICES

There are so many! How MUCH of what herb or spice should you add to WHICH dishes?????

To save you some confusion, I've compiled a simple list to help guide you through this "forest." Keep in mind that an HERB (no, NOT your brother-in-law) is basically the leaf of a temperate biennial or annual that is fragrant. SPICES come to us from the more tropical perennials, their roots, stems, fruits and leaves. The magic they possess is to aid us in accenting flavors—adding zip to a meal. But they should be used cautiously and sparingly, not because they are necessarily harmful, but because they easily can overpower. You should be familiar with them before you use them with a heavy hand, and when you do, let them "mature" before tasting (give them a chance to do their job).

Herbs and spices should be purchased in small amounts to ensure their freshness, and stored in a cool, dry area. By the way, the first recorded use of spices takes us way back to the Egyptian pyramids, thousands of years ago, when garlic and onion were used for medicinal purposes.

HERBS & SPICES GUIDELINES

SPICE/HERB	DESCRIPTION	POPULAR FORMS
Allspice	Combination flavor of cinnamon, nutmeg, cloves	Powdered
Basil	Relative of mint	Fresh or dry crushed
Bay Leaf	Woody flavor	Whole dry or powdered
Celery Seed	Aromatic seed; celery flavor	Whole or powdered
Chives	All-purpose herb; delicate onion	Dry, fresh or frozen
Cinnamon	From the cassia tree; sweet; primarily used in desserts, beverages	Powdered, sticks
Clove	Spice from buds of the clove tree; primarily used in desserts, and beverages and to add flavor to roasts	Powdered, whole
Dill	Herb; tart in flavor; used in salads, or fresh seafood	Whole, powdered
Garlic	Bulb used with meats, fish, and Italian foods	Whole fresh, powdered
Ginger	Spice of a plant root that is sweet or fresh with a biting aftertaste, used in baking and Oriental foods	Whole, powdered
Horseradish	Spicy root; turnip flavor	Fresh, bottled
Mace	Husk of nutmeg; similar mild flavor	Dried, powdered
Marjoram	Good with lamb and fowl; similar to oregano	Whole leaves, powdered
Mint	Nice with lamb and Middle Eastern or essence foods	Fresh, powdered
Nutmeg	Sweet spice	Dried seeds, powdered
Oregano	Bitter herb; great for Italian foods	Dried whole, crushed, powdered
Paprika	Ground pepper pods; nice in Hungarian dishes	Powdered
Parsley	Herb also used as a garnish	Fresh or dry
Pepper	Pungent spice; wide variety of uses	Ground, whole peppercorns
Rosemary	Lemony herb; nice with lamb and pork	Whole, dry or powdered
Sage	Lime-scented herb for poultry or stuffing	Whole dry, powdered, crushed
Shallots	Onion family	Fresh
Thyme	Versatile herb; use with meats, fish, poultry, tea flavoring	Whole or powdered

BASIC MENU IDEAS

Plan menus with nutrition in mind as well as what moves you. Think of clever ways to use leftovers. As you plan, bear in mind that a meal has to both LOOK and TASTE good or it will likely get the "upturned nose" treatment.

Remember, when the temperatures rise, appetites decrease and vice-versa! (Check the calories and nutrients. Are you getting a good balance?)

BREAKFAST

CRANBERRY JUICE

SCRAMBLED EGGS WITH ONION AND ZUCCHINI

WHOLE WHEAT OR SOURDOUGH TOAST WITH BUTTER

FRESHLY STEWED FIGS OR APRICOTS

DECAF COFFEE WITH HONEY

LOW OR NON-FAT MILK

LUNCHEON

COLD (OR WARM) VICHYSSOISE

LEAN, COLD ROAST BEEF SANDWICH ON RYE

COTTAGE CHEESE-STUFFED TOMATO

GARNISH WITH CELERY AND CARROT STICKS

HERB TEA OR LOW-FAT MILK

DINNER

BONELESS, SKINLESS CHICKEN BREASTS SAUTÉED IN

WHITE WINE, MUSHROOMS AND SOUR CREAM

BAKED POTATO WITH BUTTER AND CHIVES

VICHY CARROTS

WHOLE WHEAT ROLL AND BUTTER

WHITE WINE

FRESH FRUIT

DECAF COFFEE OR TEA, HERB TEA OR MILK

A MAN'S PLACE is in the kitchen

So, what do you think of these menus for openers? Now, it's your turn to come up with some ideas. Don't be afraid of it - GO for it!

OK, now see what **you** can come up with for the following menu planner…

BREAKFAST

A MAN'S PLACE **is in the kitchen**

LUNCHEON

A MAN'S PLACE **is in the kitchen**

DINNER

A MAN'S PLACE **is in the kitchen**

LET'S DIG IN

Now that the menu is prepared, let's have at it. But of course you'll want to be proper in setting the table. Don't panic! The old-fashioned fussiness, stuffiness and rules are gone. Naturally, formal dinners and events dictate a more formal attitude, but everyday dining should be relaxed, casual, pleasant and FUN and not exactly "slopping' the hogs." Life is already complicated with enough regulations and rules; let's not bring them to the table with us.

We've prepared a guide to help you enjoy your culinary experience. Service can either be pre-plated or family-style, with everyone serving themselves from platters and bowls at the table. To make the meal more fun, add some of these touches—you'll find they really contribute to your overall well-being and relaxation and will help transform the mere act of EATING into a very pleasant DINING EXPERIENCE.

- Use a few fresh flowers or a floral centerpiece, but avoid any with heavy fragrances.

- Use subdued lighting; light one or two candles near the center of the table (be sure to use the dripless ones.)

- Use a very plain set of china -- perhaps off-white with minimal decoration. A set of china that's embossed with a lot of pattern and/or flowers tends to be too busy and distracts from your food presentation and eye appeal.

- Use glassware that has classic lines; the simple style has a cooling and soothing effect.

- Above all, remember that the act of ingesting food should be a pleasant dining "experience" that will be remembered long after the plates are cleared. Keep conversation light and pleasant; DON'T discuss controversial topics such as politics or religion. TAKE YOUR TIME: Don't rush as if you might never eat again. Also, don't overeat! That can cause unpleasant complications and leave you with bad impressions of the moment (and a lot more calories than you need).

- After the meal, adjourn to the comfort of the living room or den for some pleasant conversation over coffee or tea, or an after-dinner cordial. Just remember the calories and consume alcohol in moderation.

- Don't immediately rush into some complex endeavor or unpleasant task; wait awhile - RELAX - savor the moment.

THE BODY TERRIFIC

"More people will die from 'hit-or-miss' eating than from 'hit-and-run' driving."
—Duncan Hines

Before you take that next bite of anything, STOP! Nothing is simpler and yet more complicated than your body; hence the requirements to keep it in optimum condition can be perplexing.

We must take a little time to understand the body's needs. We think we know what's best by allowing ourselves to be led by eye appeal, fragrances and tastes (what I call dessert for the eyes). While this works some of the time, it's not the total answer. It's easy to be fooled and led astray by Mother Nature, and very often by packaging and merchandising techniques. (Ask yourself how often the product comes out looking like the picture on the frozen TV dinner package?)

To begin, we must care about our bodies and understand their needs. The results can be phenomenal: fewer heart attacks, less obesity…the list goes on. We devote this chapter to "The Body Terrific" — its needs, the ways in which those needs can be met, and the things that should be avoided.

THE NO - NO'S
SALT

How much do you need? Well, the average American consumes two to three times the amount of sodium (salt) the body needs, in the form of good old table salt. We use it in preparation and then again when the food gets to the table — a classic case of fooling ourselves — and it can be a killer.

If you want to avoid the "sodium pit," don't use salt from the shaker or, if you must, use it sparingly. We get all the sodium our bodies need and want NATURALLY in the foods we eat: 3 to 8 grams a day is equal to about 3,000 milligrams or about a half teaspoon — and that's ALL we need. As you scan through the nutrient reference charts on pages 27-29, you'll see which foods are high in sodium. For instance, a dill pickle has 1,428 milligrams of sodium and one tablespoon of soy sauce contains 1,319 milligrams. So, as you can see, it doesn't take very long to reach your daily limit. Nutritionally speaking, salt has little or no benefit, so why not investigate some seasoning alternatives: lemon, mint, dill, pepper, onion, ginger, wine, cinnamon, basil, chives, paprika, parsley, green pepper, bay leaf, thyme, mustard, curry, garlic, tomato, oregano…the list is seemingly endless.

Now, you may ask: "Which salt is less harmful: sea salt, table salt or lite salt?" The answer is: There is no difference. Salt is salt. Lite salts contain half sodium and half potassium, which will cut down on the amount of salt you ingest, but it's expensive, so save money and cut down on your use of the salt shaker.

SUGAR

Welcome to America, the "Land of the Sweet Tooth." Many of the sweets we crave are coated with granulated sugar, (which contains about 25 calories per teaspoon and has little or no nutritional value.

Sugar seems to be everywhere. It appears naturally in foods such as fruits (which contain fructose) and is added to many packaged products; did you know that some breakfast cereals contain up to 53 percent sugar?

How can you avoid a sugar overload? You need to think about what you're eating and adjust your tastes accordingly.

Cereals are fine and tasty, but you don't have to add more sugar to enjoy them. There are many alternatives to granulated sugar, such as honey (which is high in calories but more beneficial with its trace minerals and vitamins) or molasses (which also contains important vitamins and minerals.) You can consume fresh juices instead of soda pop, and flavor foods with spices—blended or alone—such as sage, allspice, cinnamon or nutmeg.

Whatever you do, READ FOOD LABELS; you'll be amazed to learn how much sugar you are ingesting. Be aware that sugar may take many forms and can appear on labels under many names, including sucrose, fructose or corn syrup.

ADDITIVES

Artificial additives are everywhere: preservatives, flavorings, colorings, stimulants, sweeteners, antioxidants, emulsifiers, stabilizers and substitutes. Many of these are OK, but some should be used in moderation or avoided. Consider please:

CAFFEINE—A stimulant in coffee, tea and soft drinks; can be rough on the nervous system and destroys some vitamins. Limit your intake or try the decaffeinated versions. Caffeine can stimulate a rise in blood-sugar levels.

SACCHARIN—This synthetic sweetener is 350 times sweeter than sugar. Some tests have concluded it may be a contributing or causative effect for cancer. Use an alternative, such as honey or Aspartame.

SODIUM NITRATE—A preservative used in bacon, ham, sausage, hot dogs and lunch meats. Sodium nitrate can cause the production of nitrosamins (a cancer-causing chemical). Prudence should be the rule.

BROMINATED VEGETABLE OIL (BVO)—An emulsifier used in soft drinks. Residual amounts formed in body fat could be a causative influence for health issues. The best advice is moderation and prudence.

BATYLATED HYDROXYTOLUENE (BHT)—An antioxidant often found in jams, cereals and potato chips. May be a contributing cause of allergies. Use in moderation.

FOOD COLORINGS—Found in beverages, candy, bakery products, red cocktail cherries, sausage, gelatin desserts, pet foods and more. Can contain unusually high levels of iodine and carry other possible health risks. Blue #1, #2, Red #40, #3, Green #3, and Yellow #5 fall into this category. Healthy, satisfying alternatives are available—look for them.

MONOSODIUM GLUTAMATE (MSG)—Used frequently in Asian cooking. May cause headaches and chest constriction.

FATS AND CHOLESTEROL

Fats and cholesterol cause us to consider more questions: Are they necessary? Yes. But are they all alike? And are they all good?

The subject of saturated animal fats (a source of protein) can be controversial. Cholesterol is the "boogie man" of heart disease. It's a waxy substance (and, oddly enough, an essential one) found in the body's cells; it is derived from animal food sources only. This is known as dietary cholesterol, until it enters the body, at which time it becomes serum cholesterol.

Fat is necessary to our bodies, but Americans tend to eat too much of it. Fat helps the fat-soluble vitamins move around and be absorbed into our systems. Fat helps us keep warm, gives us energy and insulates the heart. There are three major classifications of fats:

- SATURATED, which increases levels of cholesterol;
- POLYUNSATURATED, which decreases those levels, and
- MONOUNSATURATED, which has little or no effect on the blood.

While the debate about fat rages on, it is generally accepted that we take in too much SATURATED fat, thus the "bad" cholesterol, and that alone (or coupled with factors such as improper diet, lack of rest, improper exercise, smoking and overuse of salt) we are probably setting ourselves up for the fall: heart attacks, strokes or hypertension.

The logical solution would be to cut back on fat intake. According to the American Heart Association, the intake of fats should be limited to about 30 percent of your daily calories and cholesterol to about 300 milligrams per day. It may seem a daunting task to figure it all out, but it really is fairly simple and, considering the alternatives, well worth the effort. Listed here are some sample sources of SATURATED fats for your consideration.

DAIRY PRODUCTS

MILK: High in cholesterol and saturated fat. Consider low-fat or non-fat.
CREAM: Heavy in cholesterol and saturated fat. Try a substitute or limit.
BUTTER: Butter is the dairy product with the highest concentration of saturated fat and cholesterol. Think about limiting or using an alternative.
CHEESE: By virtue of being whole milk products, cheeses score high in both saturated fats and cholesterol; cream cheese is exceptionally high.

MEAT PRODUCTS

RED MEATS: In this area, think LEAN. With beef, "Choice" grade cuts supply much less fat than "Prime" cuts. Lean means getting the vitamins, minerals and proteins with a minimum of saturated fats.
POULTRY: Low in saturated fats and moderately high in cholesterol; a good source of protein. Thinking about eating deep-fried chicken? Consider cooking in corn oil, safflower oil or sunflower oil—all are high in polyunsaturates.
FISH: High in dietary cholesterol, but low in saturated fats. A good source of vitamins, minerals and proteins.

SHELLFISH: Crab and shrimp are very high in cholesterol, but low in saturated fats.

OTHERS: Meat products such as luncheon meats, bacon and sausage are extremely high in saturated fats; use in moderation and remember to check labels for sodium nitrates and nitrites.

To sum it all up: CHOOSE WISELY! Take the time to make comparisons. Read labels. Think about calories, fats and cholesterol. Being healthy takes some work. Try kicking the salt habit. Moderate your alcohol intake. STOP smoking altogether if you can or at least cut down and, above all, EXERCISE. It'll take you a long way along the road to optimum health.

VITAMINS & MINERALS (Recommended Dietary Allowances - RDA)

Following are sample charts, meant strictly as a dietary reference guide.
An explanation of abbreviations is included. The lists are intended only to show average dietary needs. Contact your physician for nutritional guidelines specific to your age, sex and activity level.

(Source: Food & Nutrition Board, National Academy of Sciences and National Research Council.)

kg = kilogram	lb = pound
IU = International Unit	ug = microgram (one millionth of a gram)
g = gram	mg = milligram

INFANTS 6 mos - 1yr
Size / 20 lbs Height / 28 inches

2.0 g Protein
Fat-soluble Vitamins:
  2000 IU Vitamin A
  400 IU Vitamin D
  5 IU Vitamin E
Water-soluble Vitamins:
  35 mg Vitamin C
  0.6 mg Vitamin B6
  1.5 ug Vitamin B12
  0.5 mg Vitamin B1 (Thiamine)
  0.6 mg Vitamin B2 (Riboflavin)
  8 mg Niacin
  45 ug Folacin
Minerals:
  540 mg Calcium
  360 mg Phosphorus
  70 mg Magnesium
  15 mg Iron
  5 mg Zinc
  50 ug Iodine

CHILDREN 4 - 6yrs
Size / 44 lbs Height / 44 inches

30 g Protein
Fat-soluble Vitamins:
  250 IU Vitamin A
  400 IU Vitamin D
  9 IU Vitamin E
Water-soluble Vitamins:
  45 mg Vitamin C
  1.3 mg Vitamin B6
  2.5 ug Vitamin B12
  0.9 mg Vitamin B1 (Thiamine)
  1.0 mg Vitamin B2 (Riboflavin)
  11 mg Niacin
  200 ug Folacin
Minerals:
  800 mg Calcium
  800 mg Phosphorus
  200 mg Magnesium
  10 mg Iron
  10 mg Zinc
  90 ug Iodine

ADULT MALES 23 - 50yrs

Size / 154 lbs   Height / 70 inches

56 g Protein

Fat-soluble Vitamins:
  5000 IU Vitamin A
  200 IU Vitamin D
  15 IU Vitamin E

Water-soluble Vitamins:
  60 IU Vitamin C
  2.2 IU Vitamin B6
  3.0 ug Vitamin B12
  1.4 mg Vitamin B1 (Thiamine)
  1.6 mg Vitamin B2 (Riboflavin)
  18 mg Niacin
  400 ug Folacin

Minerals:
  800 mg Calcium
  800 mg Phosphorus
  350 mg Magnesium
  10 mg Iron
  15 mg Zinc
  150 ug Iodine

ADULT FEMALES 23 - 50yrs

Size / 120 lbs   Height / 64 inches

44 g Protein

Fat-soluble Vitamins:
  4000 IU Vitamin A
  200 IU Vitamin D
  12 IU Vitamin E

Water-soluble Vitamins:
  60 mg Vitamin C
  2.0 mg Vitamin B6
  3.0 ug Vitamin B12
  1.0 mg Vitamin B1 (Thiamine)
  1.2 mg Vitamin B2 (Riboflavin)
  13 mg Niacin
  400 ug Folacin

Minerals:
  800 mg Calcium
  800 mg Phosphorus
  300 mg Magnesium
  18 mg Iron
  15 mg Zinc
  150 ug Iodine

PROTEINS (Recommended Dietary Allowances - RDA)

Women

lbs.	grams
100	36
130	47
160	58
180	66
200	70

Men

lbs	grams
140	51
170	62
200	73
240	87
250	91

Children

age	grams
0-6mo.	13.2
1-3 yrs.	23
7-10 yrs.	34
11-14 yrs.	45
15-18 yrs.	56 male/46 female

NUTRIENT GUIDE - MILK

Cal: Calories	Prot: Protein	Carb: Carbohydrates
Calc: Calcium	Phos: Phosphorus	Pot: Potassium
Thia: Thiamine	Ribo: Riboflavin	Niac: Niacin

Product (1 cup each)	Cal.	Prot. g	Fat g	Carb. g	Calc. mg	Phos. mg	Iron mg	Sod. mg	Pot. mg	Vit A IU	Vit C mg	Thia. mg	Ribo. mg	Niac. mg
Whole milk	159	8.5	8.5	12.0	288	227	0 .1	122	351	350	0.07	0.41	0.2	2
Low-fat milk	145	10.3	4.9	19.8	352	276	0.1	150	431	200	0.10	0.52	0.2	2
Non-fat milk	88	8.8	0.2	12.5	296	233	0.1	127	355	10	0.09	0.44	0.2	2
Buttermilk	88	8.8	0.2	12.5	296	233	0.1	319	343	10	0.10	0.44	0.2	2

NUTRIENT GUIDE - PROTEINS

In addition to vegetables and fruits, some other good sources of protein, in relationship to fats and calories, are presented here for your consideration:

SOURCE	PROTEIN (grams)	CALORIES	FATS (grams)
Milk:			
Whole (1 cup)	8.5	159	8.5
Low-fat (1 cup)	10.3	145	4.9
Non-fat (1 cup)	8.8	88	0.2
Eggs (one)	6.5	82	5.8
Cheese:			
Cheddar (1 slice)	3.3	52	4.2
Cottage (1 cup)	30.6	240	9.2
Cottage (1 cup low-fat)	25	125	0.4
Swiss (1 slice)	3.9	52	3.9
American (1 slice)	3.0	48	3.9
Rice:			
Instant (1 cup)	3.6	180	Trace
White (1 cup)	4.1	223	0.2
Brown (1 cup)	4.9	232	1.2
Egg noodles (1 cup)	6.6	200	2.4
Chicken:			
Skinless light (3.5 oz)	32.0	166	3.4
Dark (3.5 oz)	38.0	176	6.3
Breast (half)	32.5	203	6.4
Drumstick (one)	33.0	235	10.2
Wing (one)	29.0	268	15.0
Turkey:			
White (3.5 oz)	33.0	175	4.0
Dark (3.5 oz)	30.0	205	8.0
Tuna:			
Water-packed (1/2 cup)	28.0	125	0.8
Oil-packed (1/2 cup)	29.0	195	8.0
Halibut (3.5 oz)	25.0	171	7.0
Salmon:			
Canned (3.5 oz)	23.0	155	7.0
Fresh (3.5 oz)	27.0	180	7.0
Filet sole (4 oz)	30.0	200	8.0
Sardines in oil (3 oz)	20.5	175	9.0
Meat:			
Lean pork chop (one)	13.3	110	6.0
Lean pork loin (2 slices)	20.0	165	9.0
Lean ham (2 slices)	22.0	159	7.5
Bacon (3 slices)	8.0	155	13.0
Sausage (3 links)	11.0	285	27.0
Lean rib roast (3 oz)	24.0	205	11.4
Lean chuck roast (3 oz)	25.0	212	12.0
Lean round steak (3 oz)	26.6	161	5.2
Lean ground beef (3 oz)	23.0	186	9.6
Lean sirloin steak (3 oz)	27.4	176	6.5
Bologna (1 slice)	4.0	85	7.0
Salami (1 slice)	7.0	135	11.0
Hot dog (one)	6.0	150	14.0

NUTRIENT GUIDE - FRESH VEGETABLES

VEGETABLE	CALORIES	PROTEIN g	CARBS. g	IRON mg	SODIUM mg	VIT. A IU	VIT.C mgs
Artichokes (1 bud)	20	2.8	9.9	1.1	30	150	8
Asparagus (1 cup)	20	2.2	3.6	0.6	1	900	26
Beans /Green (1 cup)	31	2.0	6.8	0.8	5	680	15
Beans/ Lima (1 cup)	189	12.9	33.7	4.3	2	480	29
Beets (1 cup)	54	1.9	12.2	0 .9	73	30	10
Beet greens (1 cup)	93.6	2.5	4.8	2.8	110	7400	22
Broccoli (1 cup))	40	4.8	7.0	1.2	16	3880	140
Brussels sprouts (1 cup)	56	6.5	9.9	1.7	16	810	135
Carrots (1 cup)	45	1.3	10.3	0.9	48	15230	9
Cauliflower (1 cup)	28	2.9	5.1	0.9	11	80	69
Cabbage (1 cup)	29	1.6	6.2	0.4	20	190	48
Corn (1 ear)	70	2.5	16.2	0.4	Trace	310	7
Celery (1 stalk)	7	0.4	1.6	0.1	50	110	4
Cucumber (1 cup raw)	16	0.9	3.6	1.2	6	260	12
Mushrooms (1 cup raw)	20	1.9	3.1	0.6	11	Trace	2
Onions (1 cup)	61	2.5	13.7	0.8	15	80	15
Peas (1 cup)	114	8.6	19.4	2.9	2	860	32
Parsley (1 tablespoon)	2	0.1	0.3	0.2	2	300	6
Potato (1 baked)	145	4.0	32.8	1.1	6	Trace	31
Pepper/Green (one)	36	2.0	7.9	1.1	21	690	210
Pepper/Red (one)	51	2.3	11.6	1.0	0	7300	335
Spinach (1 cup, raw)	14	1.8	2.4	1.7	39	4460	28
Spinach (1 cup, cooked)	41	5.4	6.5	4.0	90	14580	50
Squash (1 cup, acorn)	113	3.9	28.7	2.3	2	2870	27
Squash (1 cup, zucchini)	22	1.8	4.5	0.7	2	540	16
Turnips (1 cup)	36	1.8	11.3	0.6	53	Trace	34

NUTRIENT GUIDE - FRESH FRUITS

FRUIT	CALS.	PROT. g	CARBS. g	IRON mg	SODIUM mg	VIT. A IU	VIT. C mg	OTHER
Avocado (one)	376	4.8	14.2	1.4	10	330	16	HIGH FAT
Apples (one)	96	0.3	24.0	1.0	2	150	7	
Apricots (three)	55	1.1	13.7	1.0	1	2890	11	
Bananas (one)	101	1.3	26.4	0.8	1	230	12	HIGH POTASSIUM
Figs (one)	40	0.6	10.2	3	1	40	1	
Cherries (1 cup)	82	1.5	20.4	0.5	2	130	12	
Grapes (1 cup)	70	1.3	15.9	4.0	3	100	4	
Grapefruit (half)	40	0.5	10.3	0.4	1	80	37	
Pineapple (1 cup)	81	0.6	21.2	0.8	2	110	26	
Mango (one)	152	1.6	38.8	0.9	16	11090	81	RDA VIT. A
Cantaloupe (1 cup)	48	1.1	12.0	0.6	1.9	5440	53	
Oranges (one)	64	1.3	16.0	0.5	1	260	66	
Nectarine (one)	88	0.8	23.6	0.7	8	2280	18	
Peaches (one)	38	0.6	9.7	0.5	1	1330	7	GOOD VIT.A
Papaya (one)	119	1.8	30.4	0.9	9	5320	170	
Pears (one)	100	1.1	25.1	0.5	3	30	7	
Raspberries (1 cup)	700	1.5	16.7	1.1	1	160	31	
Strawberries (1 cup)	55	1.0	12.5	1.5	1	940	11	
Tomato (one, raw)	19	1.0	4.1	0.4	3	790	20	
Watermelon (1 cup)	42	0.8	10.2	0.7	8	2280	1	

TEST YOURSELF

There are no failures here, so don't fear it if you "flunk" this test. Simply skim back through what you've read in this book and try again—you'll likely do much better.

For every correct answer, award yourself 5 points; for each incorrect answer, subtract 5 points. In the end, rank your test score as follows: 100 points is excellent, 75 points is good, 50 points is OK; 25 points is "so-so," 10 points or fewer and you'd better do some re-reading. Do yourself a favor and don't sneak any peeks—you'll be amazed by how much you've learned.

1. Is table salt really necessary to our bodies? If so, how much?

2. Which salt is less harmful: sea salt, table salt or lite salt?

3. List two alternatives to salt.

4. Sodium nitrite is a coloring agent used in fruits: True or False

5. It's not necessary to real labels; the federal government makes sure everything is correct: True or False

6. How many grams of protein does the average 30-year-old male need daily?

7. Everyone requires the same amount of vitamin A daily: True or False

8. Mg. stands for microgram: True or False

9. Carrots are high in Vitamin A: True or False

10. Asparagus is extremely high in sodium content, and should be avoided: True or False

11. Mangos are the best fruit source of Vitamin A with 11,090 IU per unit: True or False

12. How many calories are there in a cup of whole milk?

13. What is the best overall type of cookware?

14. What is meant by the term "blanch?"

15. "Al Dente" is an Italian chef from New York: True or False.

16. What is the equivalent of 1 fluid ounce?

17. A"moderate" oven is what temperature?

18. One pound of raisins is equal to how many cups?

19. Describe the difference between herbs and spices.

20. What spice is used heavily in Asian cooking?

TEST ANSWERS ON PAGE 169

APPETIZERS:
bites & nibbles

"We may live without friends; we may live without books;
but civilized man cannot live without cooks."
—Edward Robert Bulwer-Lytton

Appetizers and hors d'oeuvres can best be described as a way of tempting the taste buds for what is to follow. Basically, appetizers are finger foods or small plated items— snippets of satiation—perhaps to accompany a glass of wine or cocktail, and certainly not meant as an entree. Generally allow for about 12 pieces per person at a cocktail party.

Appetizers are terrific fare for holiday or cocktail party entertaining. They can be served hot or cold, and come in a huge variety.

I could devote an entire delicious volume to the "Appetizer," but much as they are meant to tempt, so shall I—with but a few.

QUICHE

3 eggs, well beaten	1 1/2 cups heavy cream
Salt to taste	Freshly ground pepper to taste
24 mini tart shells	4 ounces ham, finely chopped
6 ounces mild cheese, grated	1/2 small onion, minced

Yes, real men do eat quiche, or they should if they have any smarts at all!

Preheat the oven to 375 degrees. Whisk together eggs, cream, salt and pepper and transfer to a glass measuring cup for easy pouring. Place the tart shells about an inch apart on a cookie sheet. Distribute the ham, cheese and onion evenly into the bottom of the shells leaving top half of the shell empty. Fill each (not to the tip-top) with the egg/cream mixture. Bake 20 to 25 minutes until egg mixture is firm and tops are golden brown. (The quiches are done when a toothpick inserted into the center comes out clean.) Serve warm with wine or a cocktail.

Yield: 6 to 8 appetizer servings

VEGETABLE STIR 'N BAKE

1 large Walla Walla or Vidalia onion, chopped

2 tablespoons virgin olive oil	Finely minced garlic to taste
Dash sweet basil	Dash oregano
Salt to taste	Black pepper to taste
1 to 2 tomatoes, coarsely chopped	8 ounces baby white mushrooms, whole

6 medium zucchini, coarsely chopped

1 to 2 cups your favorite shredded cheese(s)

Optional:

Add leftover shredded pork or chicken, cooked ground beef or shrimp to taste

This can be served as a light buffet item, heavy appetizer or entree!

In a large skillet, sauté chopped onion in oil until it is soft and translucent. Add to this finely minced garlic, a dash each of sweet basil and oregano, and salt and pepper to taste. Add chopped tomatoes (if possible, use freshly picked), mushrooms and chopped zucchini. Stir to blend the mixture. Reduce heat and simmer (barely bubble) uncovered for about 15 minutes, stirring occasionally. While this mixture is cooking, lightly grease a medium baking dish, and pre-heat the oven to 350 degrees. When it's ready, transfer the tomato mixture to the baking dish and top with a generous portion of your favorite cheese (or cheeses). Bake 10 to 15 minutes or until the cheese is melted and bubbly. (This is a marvelous vegetarian dish, or you may choose to add meat to the dish while baking.) Serve with rice or another starch and thick slices of warm, buttered French bread. Top it all off with fresh fruit for dessert and a glass of iced tea. *Ummm Ummmm, it's sheer ambrosia! Now that wasn't too difficult, was it?*

Yield: 12 to 20 appetizer/buffet servings or 4 to 6 entree servings.

CRISPY ZUCCHINI BITES

6 large zucchini	1 cup milk
1 cup flour	2 eggs, lightly beaten
1 clove garlic, minced	1 tablespoon water
1/4 cup bacon drippings (adding more as needed)	
Salt or celery salt to taste	Black pepper to taste
Dash Tabasco (optional)	

Slice zucchini (tips removed) lengthwise into 1/4 inch strips. Dip the strips in milk, then in flour to cover. Dip the strips again in a lightly beaten mixture of egg, garlic and water; dip in flour again. Gently sauté in bacon drippings until golden brown (just a few minutes each side); drain on paper towels and sprinkle with desired seasonings. (If you really want to bump up the spice, add a touch of Tabasco to the egg mix.) Can be served as an appetizer or as a veggie side dish.

Yield: 12 to 20 appetizer or 6 side dish servings.

Variation

6 large zucchini	2 tablespoons Worcestershire sauce
1/2 cup virgin olive oil	1/8 cup tarragon vinegar
2 cloves garlic, finely minced	
Salt to taste	Black pepper to taste

Slice zucchini (tips removed) lengthwise into 1/4 inch strips. Marinate (soak) the zucchini for 1 hour in a mixture of Worcestershire sauce, olive oil, tarragon vinegar and garlic and your favorite seasonings (try Spike Seasoning Mix). Grill zucchini over a low charcoal fire, brushing zucchini with the marinade while grilling. Grill a couple minutes on each side or until crisp. Zucchini cooks quickly, so watch cooking time. *Very tasty indeed!*

Yield: 12 to 20 appetizer or 6 side dish servings.

CORTON (Pork Pate Français Canadien)

2 pounds pork butt, ground twice – (very fine)*	
5 cups water	1 small onion, minced
1/2 cup celery, diced	2 teaspoons salt
1/2 teaspoon black pepper	1 teaspoon ground cinnamon
1/2 teaspoon ground cloves	

* Most butchers or grocery store meat counters will be happy to accommodate your request for double grinding.

Combine all ingredients in a large pot and bring to a boil. Reduce heat and simmer (barely bubbling) uncovered for 2 to 2 1/2 hours or until liquid is gone, mashing frequently with a potato masher. Chill thoroughly overnight. Use as a pate on crackers or fresh, heated, crusty French bread, perhaps topped with a dab of Dijon Mustard, or shaved raw onion. A bit fattening, but VERY tasty!

Yield: About 2 quarts.

ESCARGOT BOURGUIGNONNE

2 dozen snails*	1 cup butter, softened
1 teaspoon onion, minced	1 clove garlic, minced
1 tablespoon parsley, chopped	Salt to taste
Black pepper to taste	1/4 cup breadcrumbs

To save time, use canned snails, already cleaned and ready to cook. Buy the shells (which are sold separately) which can be cleaned and reused. Oven snail dishes are easily obtainable, and go from oven to table; or the snails may be baked in a small baking dish.

Preheat the oven to 400 degrees. Combine butter, onion, garlic, parsley, salt and pepper in a small mixing bowl, and blend thoroughly. Put a bit of the butter mixture in the bottom of each snail shell, then place a snail in each shell and fill the remainder of the shell with the butter mixture. Arrange the shells (bottom down) on the snail dish or baking dish and sprinkle with the breadcrumbs. Bake uncovered for about 10 minutes and serve very hot with crusty French bread.
Yield: 4 appetizer servings.

COQUILLES ST. JACQUES à la PARISIENNE

1 1/2 pounds fresh sea scallops
1 1/2 cup dry white wine
Salt to taste
Black pepper to taste
3 tablespoons butter
1 cup heavy cream
2 tablespoons all-purpose flour
1/2 cup white button mushrooms, chopped
2 tablespoons breadcrumbs
2 tablespoons Swiss cheese, grated

While a bit on the rich side, this is an elegant way to begin that "special" meal.

Combine scallops, wine, salt and pepper in a heavy saucepan, and slowly bring to a boil. Reduce heat, simmer for 5 minutes and drain (setting the drained cooking liquid aside). Carefully cut the hot scallops into bite-size pieces and set aside. Heat 1 1/2 tablespoons of the butter in the saucepan until melted. Add the reserved liquid from before and the heavy cream and stir constantly, blending in flour a little at a time until desired consistency is reached (about 5 minutes). Add the mushrooms and scallops, and continue cooking another 5 minutes, stirring occasionally. Season to taste. Spray coquille shells (which are available in department, specialty or gourmet stores) with cooking spray; in lieu of these shells, use individual ramekins or soufflé dishes. Fill the shells with the scallop mixture and sprinkle with breadcrumbs, dotting the tops with the remaining 1 1/2 tablespoons butter and cheese. Broil until browned. Wonderful with a glass of chilled dry white wine.
Yield: 4 to 6 appetizer or luncheon servings.

CRUDITE NIPPON

4 cucumbers, sliced	4 cups carrot sticks
4 cups cauliflower florets	4 cups broccoli florets
4 cups celery chunks	4 cups cherry tomatoes

1 8-ounce can water chestnuts, slice in half
Soy sauce (enough to cover cucumbers)

Dip Ingredients:

2 cups mayonnaise	2 cups sour cream
2 tablespoons hot mustard	1 teaspoon Worcestershire sauce
1/2 teaspoon garlic powder	1/2 tablespoon curry powder

Prepare veggies (you may consider using others such as zucchini, radishes or mushrooms) and chill. Using a fork, score the length of the cucumbers, then slice, marinate and chill the cucumbers in soy sauce for a half hour. Blend together dip ingredients; season to taste. Chill the dip for 30 minutes. Drain the soy sauce from the cucumbers, and arrange them with other veggies on a serving platter, placing the dip in the center. Provide toothpicks and napkins.
Yield: 20 to 30 appetizer servings.

RUMAKI

1 cup dry cooking wine
1 tablespoon soy sauce
1 clove garlic, minced
1 tablespoon brown sugar
Ground ginger to taste
1 pound fresh chicken livers, halved (about 24 pieces),
rinsed and drained
8 water chestnuts, each slivered into 3 slices (about 24 pieces)
1/2 pound bacon strips, halved (about 24 pieces)

Mix wine, soy sauce, garlic, brown sugar and ginger; marinate refrigerated chicken livers in this mixture for several hours, but preferably overnight. After marinating, reserve the mixture. When ready to prepare, preheat the oven to 400 degrees. Make a tiny slit in each liver piece and insert a water chestnut sliver; roll the liver in a slice of the bacon and secure with a toothpick. In an oven-proof pan, roast the rumaki uncovered for 45 minutes, basting occasionally with the marinade, and draining any buildup of the bacon fat drippings. When done, the rumaki will be nicely browned and glazed.
Yield: 6 to 12 appetizer servings.

GUACAMOLE

4 ripe avocados, halved lengthwise
2 tablespoons onion, minced
1 small tomato, diced
1 clove garlic, minced
2 tablespoons lemon juice
1 tablespoon virgin olive oil
1/4 cup mayonnaise
Salt to taste
Dash red pepper

Remove pits from halved avocados and scoop avocado meat into a bowl. Use a fork to mash the avocado. Blend all the other ingredients well with the avocado; cover and chill for at least an hour before serving. Serve with warm tortilla chips at a cocktail party or as a starter before dinner.
Yield: 2 pints dip.

MARINATED CHILLED SHRIMP

3 cloves garlic, peeled and slightly crushed
4 tablespoons lemon juice
2 cup balsamic vinaigrette
Salt to taste
Black pepper to taste
Finely chopped parsley to taste
1 pound medium (30 to 40 count) cooked shrimp, deveined, shelled and tails removed
Lemon slices
Lettuce leaves
Crushed ice

Prepare the marinade by blending garlic, lemon juice, vinaigrette, salt and pepper and parsley to taste. Add the shrimp and toss to coat well; chill shrimp and marinate for 5 to 6 hours, tossing occasionally. When ready to serve, remove the shrimp from the marinade. Present the shrimp on a bed of lettuce atop crushed ice and surrounded by lemon wedges. *These will go fast!*
Yield: 30 to 40 shrimp.

SOUPS:
slurping sensations

> "The proof of the pudding is in the eating;
> by a small sample we may judge the whole piece."
> —Miguel de Cervantes

There are soups in cans and soups in packages, cold soups and hot soups, thin soups and thick soups, meat soups and poultry soups, fruit soups and creamed soups, pasta soups and seafood soups, wine soups and vegetable soups. There are soups to start the meal, and soups that are the meal. There are soups for winter and soups for summer, won-ton soups and gazpachos, soups made with turtle or pumpkin or chestnuts.

The ethnic varieties and combinations seem to be endless and staggering.

The complexities of soup tend to be intimidating, sending many of us straight for the can or package. After all, it's easier and just as good—right? WRONG! A can of soup, while adequate, can hardly be classified as creative, fun or overly nutritious. Many prepared soups are loaded with sodium, sugar and preservatives.

So, what to do? Well, first and foremost, get over the fear and intimidation; and then, try the alternative...Egad, that means HOMEMADE SOUP!

BASIC SOUP TYPES

There are only four basic categories of soup: thin and clear, hearty (seafood, meat or vegetable), creamed, and dessert (sweet or fruity).

From these basic groups come all the variables: consommés, chowders, potages, veloutés, bisques and bouillons. I've endeavored to familiarize you with the types of soups, their preparation and service, by preparing the following chart:

SOUP TYPES						
SOUP TYPE	**BASIC INGREDIENTS**	**CONSISTENCY**	**COURSE**	**PREPARATION**	**GARNISH**	**SERVICE**
Chowder	Shellfish, fish, veggies, milk	Rich/creamy	Main/1st	Simmer	Dill, chive, parsley	Soup plate
Consommé	Meat or poultry broth	Rich, clarified	1st	Simmer, clarify, strain	Croutons	Bouillon cup
Stew	Beef, veggies	Hearty	Main	Simmer	Grated cheese	Soup plate
Chicken Noodle	Chicken, veggies, noodles	Thin to hearty	Main/1st	Simmer	Grated cheese	Soup plate
French Onion	Onions	Thin to hearty	1st	Simmer	Grated cheese, croutons	Double bouillon bowl
Cream of Vegetable	Veggies, eggs, cream	Rich	1st	Simmer & puree	Parsley	Soup plate

HELPFUL SOUP HINTS

1) Make soups well in advance so flavors blend well. Then cool and reheat prior to serving.

2) Hot soups should be served VERY hot in heated bowls.

3) Cold soups should be served WELL CHILLED in chilled bowls.

4) The flavor (in chilled soups) can sometimes be affected; you may have to adjust seasonings to taste.

5) Make soup using the water from cooked veggies (loaded with nutrients, AND delicious.)

BEEF STEW

    1 1/2 to 2 pounds lean stew beef, cut into bite-size cubes
    1/2 cup virgin olive oil
Fresh vegetables, all washed, prepared, and cut into bite-size pieces:
    1 pound carrots
    1 bunch celery
    1 large onion
    1 green pepper
    6 potatoes
    1 turnip
    2 cloves garlic, minced
    8 ounces fresh white button mushrooms, whole
    Water (to cover and cook vegetables)
    Salt to taste
    Black pepper to taste
Frozen vegetables, to be added later:
    1 9-ounce package peas
    1 9-ounce package green beans
    1 29-ounce can crushed tomatoes
    2 14-ounce cans vegetable consommé
    1 cup dry red wine
    Sweet basil to taste
    Oregano to taste
    1 bay leaf

> *This is, and always shall be one of my favorites - a great meal, loaded with vitamins and minerals, and on a cold winter day, something to look forward to. Thanks, Mom!*

Place carrots, onion, turnip, pepper, potatoes, garlic and celery in a large soup or stock pot; add just enough water to cover. Bring water to a boil, then lower heat to simmer (barely bubble) soup; cover and stir frequently. Meanwhile, place oil in a large skillet over medium heat; add cubed meat a bit at a time and brown evenly on all sides. As meat pieces finish, drain with a slotted spoon, and put them in the soup pot. (*Should you suddenly get the urge for a chicken soup instead, substitute cooked chicken meat for the beef—Presto! It's now chicken soup.*) After all browned meat has been moved to soup pot, add the bay leaf, oregano, basil, salt and pepper. Continue to simmer soup, covered, for about an hour. Then add consommé, tomatoes, red wine, mushrooms, peas and green beans. Continue to stir frequently, tasting and adjusting the seasonings as needed. Simmer covered for another hour or more, until meat and veggies are tender, and the flavors are blended.

> *Ideally, this is best served the next day—it's outrageous! While this is called a "stew," it is actually a soup. For those who prefer a true stew, this could be thickened to preference. And if there are other veggies you like (zucchini, etc.) throw them in the pot. With fresh bread and butter: ambrosia!*

Yield: 12+ entree servings.

MUSHROOM VEGETABLE & RICE SOUP

4 cups prepared white rice
3 tablespoons virgin olive oil
1/2 pound cooked snow peas
2 small onions, diced
1 clove garlic, minced
1 46-ounce can vegetable consommé
2 carrots, diced
2 stalks celery, diced
Salt to taste
Black pepper to taste
1 8-ounce package fresh white button mushrooms, sliced

Set prepared rice and snow peas aside. In a small skillet, sauté the onion and garlic in olive oil, until onion is glassy and garlic is golden; In a soup pot, combine consommé, carrots, celery and the onion and garlic, and bring to a boil; lower heat to simmer (soup will be barely boiling) and cook about 10 minutes or until vegetables are al dente (tender but not overcooked). Taste; add salt and pepper as needed. Add mushrooms and snow peas and continue heating another 5 minutes. Add the rice, stir and continue to heat through. Great on a cool day.
Yield: 6 to 8 starter servings.

GROENTENSOEP (Green Soup)

2 leeks, chopped
1 1/2 cups celery, diced
1/2 cup carrots, diced
1 cup peas, pureed
1 cup green beans
1/2 cup cauliflower florets
4 tablespoons butter
3 14-ounce cans chicken or vegetable stock
1/8 cup parsley, finely chopped
1/8 cup scallions, finely chopped
1/8 cup celery leaf, finely chopped
1 clove garlic, minced
Salt to taste
Black pepper to taste

This is a delicious favorite of mine from many Scandinavian trips, and while "Green Soup" doesn't sound all that appetizing, it is addictive and simple to prepare.

Rinse and drain all veggies (except the peas) and lightly toss in melted butter in a large soup pan until coated. Add stock, chopped parsley, scallions, celery leaf, garlic, salt and pepper and bring it to a boil. Immediately reduce heat to low and simmer (barely bubbling) for 15 minutes, or until veggies are just tender. Add the pureed peas during the last 5 minutes. Serve very hot. This light veggie soup will be a hit with your family.
Yield: 6 to 8 starter servings.

QUICK CREAMY PEA SOUP

    5 cups canned peas, drained
    1/2 cup parsley, chopped
    1/2 small onion, minced
    2 1/2 cups chicken broth
    1/2 cup heavy cream
    Salt to taste
    Black pepper to taste

In a blender, puree peas, parsley and onion; slowly add 1 1/4 cups of the broth; transfer to a medium saucepan. Slowly add the remaining 1 1/4 cups broth and cook covered over low to medium heat for 10 to 15 minutes. Reduce heat; add the cream and season to taste with the salt and pepper. Simmer (barely bubble) soup another 5 minutes until thoroughly heated. Ideal with warm sourdough bread.
Yield: 4 to 6 starter servings.

POTATO SOUP SUISSE

    6 slices bacon, crumbled
    2 small onions, diced
    4 potatoes, cooked and diced (about 4 cups)
    2 tablespoons butter
    1/2 teaspoon nutmeg
    1 teaspoon Worcestershire sauce
    6 cups milk or cream
    1 cup Swiss cheese, grated
    Salt to taste
    Black pepper to taste

In a large sauté pan, fry bacon until crisp and remove from the pan to drain on paper towels. Keep a small amount of the bacon fat in the pan and sauté the onion until glassy. In a medium-large sauce pan, add the potatoes (just slightly "smashed"), butter, half the bacon, onions, nutmeg, and Worcestershire sauce. Stir in 1 cup of the milk or cream, and heat slowly over low heat. Gradually stir in the remaining milk or cream until thoroughly heated. During the last few moments, add in half of the grated cheese and season to taste. Serve topped with a bit of the remaining cheese and bacon.
Yield: 6 to 8 starter servings.

CHILLED ALMOND SOUP

1 onion, finely chopped
2 cloves garlic, minced
2 stalks celery, chopped fine
Dash sea salt
1/2 teaspoon black pepper
2 to 3 tablespoons virgin olive oil
1 tablespoon almond extract (or to taste)
3 1/2 cups water
1/2 teaspoon nutmeg
Dash cinnamon
1 1/2 cups 2 percent milk or heavy cream
1/4 to 1/2 cup slivered roasted almonds (for garnish)
1/4 cup fresh parsley, chopped (for garnish)

In a medium skillet, sauté onion, garlic, celery, sea salt and pepper in oil until onions are transparent and just beginning to brown. Add almond extract and continue to sauté, stirring constantly for 1 to 2 minutes. Add water, nutmeg and cinnamon; continue to sauté for 1 minute. Remove from the heat; when cool, pour into blender and "pulse" puree on low just briefly while slowly adding milk or cream. Thoroughly chill and serve topped with slivered almonds and parsley.
Yield: 4 to 6 starter servings.

CHILLED CUCUMBER SOUP

5 tablespoons virgin olive oil
2 onions, finely chopped
3 cucumbers, peeled, seeded and finely chopped
Dash salt
Dash sweet basil
1/4 teaspoon freshly ground black pepper
2 cups water
2 cups 2 percent milk or cream
2 tablespoons Wondra quick-mix flour
4 tablespoons fresh chives, chopped

Heat olive oil in large sauté pan; add onions and cucumbers, cooking for approximately 5 minutes until the onion is translucent and lightly browned. Add salt, sweet basil, and pepper. Stir while adding water and milk or cream; return to simmer; gradually blend in flour until just slightly thickened. Remove from heat and let cool. Pour soup into a blender and "pulse" puree. Thoroughly chill; serve topped with fresh chopped chives.
Yield: 4 luncheon servings.

POT-AU-FEU

4 pounds soup bones
4 pounds rump roast
2 tablespoons salt
1 small bunch celery
2 cloves garlic, minced
2 bay leaves
Black pepper to taste
5 quarts water (add more as needed)
1 large onion, cut into 8 large chunks
6 to 8 small whole potatoes, peeled
1 pound fresh carrots, cut into large pieces
1 turnip, peeled and diced
8 leeks (whites only)
8 ounces white button mushrooms, whole

This is a variation of a French national treasure, a hearty soup that is a wonderful main course served with warmed French bread on a cool winter night.

Place beef bones, beef, salt, cleaned leafy celery tops, garlic, bay leaves, and pepper in a large soup or stock pot; cover with water. Bring soup to a boil, then lower heat and simmer (barely bubble) for 1 1/2 to 2 hours, using a long-handled cooking spoon to frequently skim off the surface residue. While soup is simmering, prepare all the vegetables: peel and cut the turnip into desired chunks, remove the tops and tips from carrots, brush with a veggie brush, and cut into large pieces. Cut the bottom off the celery bunch and discard (the leafy tops should already be in the pot with the beef); cut the remaining celery into large chunks. Cut the root-ends off the leeks, and slice the white portion of the leeks into large segments. Peel and rinse potatoes and leave whole; rinse mushrooms and leave whole. After reaching the appropriate cooking time, remove the bones from the soup pot and again skim off the fat; add all the veggies. Again bring to a boil adding additional water as needed, then reduce heat and simmer for another 1 to 1 1/2 hours, tasting and correcting seasonings. Remove the bay leaf prior to serving. There are a couple of ways to serve this dish. Many of the French prefer to eat the beef sliced and with the veggies as a main course, and the bouillon or broth served as a preliminary soup. Others like the beef thinly sliced or chunked and returned to the pot, to be served as a hearty main course soup. Whichever way best serves your purpose, we think you'll agree this really is a treasure.
Yield: 12+ entree servings.

CHILLED TOMATO SOUP

4 tablespoons virgin olive oil
1 large onion, finely chopped
2 to 3 cloves garlic, minced
Dash celery seed
1/2 teaspoon salt
1/4 teaspoon black pepper
Dash oregano (optional)
2 teaspoons sweet basil
1 29-ounce can tomatoes, chopped and kitchen-ready
1 cup tomato-based vegetable juice
Up to 2 tablespoons Wondra quick-mix flour
1 to 2 cups pre-cooked orzo or pastine pasta (optional)

Heat oil in large sauté pan; cook onion and garlic (vary amount according to your tastes) until onion is translucent and just beginning to brown. Add celery seed, salt, pepper, oregano (optional) and sweet basil as you sauté. Add tomatoes and vegetable juice and simmer for 10 minutes. While simmering, dust soup with quick-mixing flour and stir until just SLIGHTLY thickened. Remove from heat and let cool. Add pre-cooked pastine or orzo (optional) and thoroughly chill. Wonderful served with warm sourdough bread. (Also great heated, if you prefer.)
Yield: 4 to 6 starter servings.

VICHYSSOISE FRANÇAISE

2 to 3 pounds potatoes, diced medium
6 large onions (or 4 to 6 bunches leeks), diced
1 teaspoon black pepper
1/2 teaspoon salt
4 cloves garlic, minced
4 29-ounce cans beef consommé (or substitute chicken broth or half of each)
Water as necessary to cover
4 cups heavy cream
1/2 pound creamery butter
1/2 cup fresh parsley, finely chopped

Place potatoes, onions (or leeks), pepper, salt and garlic in a large stock pot. Cover with consommé or broth and water as needed, and bring to a boil; reduce heat and simmer covered until fully cooked, but not mushy. The liquid should be cooked down to about half. DO NOT DRAIN. Slightly "smash" with a potato masher; add cream and butter. Return to simmer while continuously stirring until butter is melted and soup is very hot. Top with parsley and serve with warm, crusty French bread and butter. A hearty meal in itself.
Yield: 12+ entree servings.

POTAGE à la ONION FRANÇAIS CANADIEN

2 tablespoons creamery butter
6 large onions, thinly shaved
Freshly ground black pepper, to taste
2 cloves garlic, minced
3 14-ounce cans beef consommé
2 cups water
Wondra quick-mix flour as needed
1/2 cup heavy cream
4 to 6 tablespoons Parmesan cheese
2 cups croutons

Melt butter in large sauté pan; cook onions, pepper, salt and garlic (vary amount according to your taste), until onions are translucent and just browned. Transfer to a medium to large soup pot. Cover with consommé and water; blend in just enough Wondra to thicken slightly. Simmer for about 20 minutes; slowly add the cream and continue heating until very hot (but not boiling). Serve topped with cheese and croutons.
Yield: 6 to 8 starter servings.

BLACK & RED BEAN SOUP

3 cups water (more as needed)
2 14-ounce cans black beans, drained
1 14-ounce can red beans, drained
1/4 teaspoon salt
1/2 teaspoon black pepper
2 cups smoked ham, diced
1 medium onion, diced
1 large carrot, diced
1 29-ounce can tomatoes, diced kitchen ready
1 14-ounce can pork and beans (yep!)

In water, cook red and black beans, salt and pepper over low heat until tender (about 10 to 15 minutes). Do not drain. Add ham, onion, carrot, tomatoes and pork and beans. Adjust seasonings and simmer (adding additional water as necessary for desired consistency) covered for 1/2 hour or until done to taste. (*Was this designed in Heaven, or what?*)
Yield: 4 to 6 starter servings.

HAM, RICE & LEMON SOUP

6 tablespoons butter
2 cups leeks, chopped
1 clove garlic, minced
Salt to taste
Black pepper to taste
6 cups chicken broth
1/2 cup uncooked long-grain rice
12 cooked asparagus spears, chopped in bite-size pieces
Water as necessary
2 cups cooked ham, diced
3 tablespoons lemon juice
2 teaspoons orange zest (grated rind)

Melt butter in large sauté pan over medium heat; sauté leeks and garlic (add salt and pepper) for about 5 minutes. Add broth and rice and bring to a boil. Cover and reduce heat to simmer (barely bubble) soup for another 15 minutes. Add asparagus and continue simmering covered for another 5 to 10 minutes, adding water as needed. Add ham, juice and zest and heat thoroughly. Adjust seasonings if necessary.
Yield: 4 to 6 starter servings.

POTATO & LEEK SOUP

2 tablespoons virgin olive oil
1 medium onion, diced
1 carrot, diced
4 leeks (2 to 3 inches before trimming), chopped
4 stalks celery, diced
2 cloves garlic, minced
6 large potatoes, peeled and cubed
2 1/2 quarts chicken or vegetable stock
8 ounces plain yogurt
1/2 teaspoon black pepper, for garnish
Fresh chives, chopped for garnish

Heat oil in a large soup kettle or stock pot; sauté onions, carrots, leeks, celery and garlic until just tender and wilted, but not browned. Add the potatoes and the chicken or vegetable stock, and bring to a boil. Reduce heat and simmer 7 to 10 minutes, stirring occasionally. Remove from the heat. Remove and puree the vegetables in a food processor or blender in small batches. When finished pureeing, return to soup kettle and add the yogurt a bit at a time, until blended. If soup has cooled, reheat very gently—do not boil. When the desired temperature is reached, serve topped with pepper and chive garnish. Serve with warmed farm-style bread.
Yield: 8 to 10 starter servings

SALADS:
beyond backyard greens

"Be yourself - no one can ever tell you're doing it wrong."
—James Leo Herlihy

The "World of Salads" is truly one of the more exciting aspects of food preparation...I should say, it CAN be. The typical limp lettuce leaf, drenched in dressing and sporting an occasional mushy slice of what was once a tomato, is often served under the heading of "Salad." If this has been your lot, read on.

The salad dates back to the days of the Roman Empire. It's as varied as the seasons and limited only by your imagination. Almost ANY edible is eligible to grace the salad-maker's table, such as:

- Salads made from a variety of greens as a base
- Fresh fruit salads
- Salads prepared with a pasta base
- Fresh vegetable salads
- Meat, fish or poultry salads
- Meats with greens
- Meats and vegetables with greens
- Fresh fruits with greens
- Fresh shellfish and seafood with greens and/or pasta

Indeed, the combinations seem endless. Any ideas of your own? The basic secret to the best salads are the "base" greens. When we think of salads, most of us revert to that venerable, if overused old standby: Iceberg lettuce. It's always prominent in stores and has gained a traditional place as an American staple. Remember, however that there are many other greens that are absolutely wonderful as salad bases, with considerably better flavors and nutritional content. It seems too few of us try them, but seem content to stay with the status quo. *(I recall someone once asking a waiter for "minimal lettuce," to which the waiter replied: "I'm sorry but we only have Iceberg.")*

Following are some examples of fabulous salad greens:

Boston or Butter lettuce: a wonderfully flavored loose leaf of buttery texture.

Bibb lettuce: a small, pale green to medium green variety of very subtle flavor.

Romaine lettuce: high in vitamin content, green and ultra-crispy.

Watercress: dark green, piquant leaves; high in vitamins and great when mixed with other greens.

Cabbage: High in vitamin C.
Dates back to the Romans and Greeks.

Spinach: Very high in iron and vitamins A and C.

Endive: A favorite of the early Egyptians. Endive is a "bitter herb" that God commanded the Israelites to eat at Passover.

HOW, WHEN & WHY?

Consider combinations and experiment! Purchase greens when firm and not wilted, yellowed or blemished. As soon as possible, greens should be trimmed of undesirable leaves and stems, washed and refrigerated to maintain their vitality.

Greens should be thoroughly rinsed in cold water, well-drained and blotted; then wrapped in toweling or plastic wrap and refrigerated. Stemmed greens should have their stems removed, leaves thoroughly rinsed, then be blotted dry on paper toweling before refrigerating. For head lettuce (such as Iceberg), cut out the stem base and rinse (holding the head so that cold water is forced into the stem opening and leaves), and then drain on paper toweling with cut end down until fairly dry; wrap as above and refrigerate.

OK, so now we've purchased, cleaned and stored the base greens; what other considerations, implications and combinations will go into our eventual creation? There are a few more points to ponder before we "go at it." For instance:

What kind of a bowl do I use?
For total success, I feel the best bowl is glass, and not the proverbial, well-seasoned wooden bowl. Bacteria can and will build up in the tiny crevices with a residue that's sure to be rancid. The glass (plastic is also usable) bowl should be large enough to accommodate all the ingredients, so that they don't end up in a 50-yard pass to the opposite end of the kitchen while they're being tossed.

How much salad do I prepare?
Quite simply, prepare only what is to be eaten immediately. Not only do prepared foods lose nutrients rapidly, but leftover, limp salad is hardly palatable (indeed, it is no longer salad).

When should I prepare the salad?
Nutrients are lost through cut surfaces, so salads should be prepared just prior to consumption.

Can salads be served as a main course or in a sandwich?
But of course! Read on—you'll find ultra-delicious, healthy and filling main course salads, and salads for sandwiches. (Try loading your salad into pita bread, the pocket-bread that is a staple of the Middle East.)

How can I be sure that my salad is nutritious AND tasty?
First of all, "tasty" is not always synonymous with "nutritious." Remembering those herbs and spices, will surely add zip to a bland salad, while retaining nutrition.

Well now, after reading up a bit on the "How, When and Why?" of salads, you can see the miracle of combinations that will give you the best source of vitamins and other nutrients, colors and flavors.

For those who may be dieting, you'll be able to build great main course salads that are highly nutritional and appetizing. It's easy once you get the hang of it.

Greens are not always the highest source of nutrients, but the items used to "dress up" the salad often can be. Try using the darkest, deepest greens as they are the highest in nutritional value. A good salad is a subtle combination—a contrast in textures and flavors.

Also remember: a plate of lettuce is NOT a salad, so use those "dress-up" items! You have tons from which to choose. Consider adding any of these items to take your salad from ordinary to extraordinary: cucumbers, carrots, mushrooms, cauliflower, turnips, celery, zucchini, cheese, meats, eggs, nuts, seeds, fresh fruits and seafood. (Hold on a minute; whatever became of that old friend, the venerable tomato?) Well, usually, they're so juicy, that to mix them into the salad with all the other "dress-ups," is to risk having a soggy mess.

Alas, all is not lost; if we opt to be traditional, we may surely use the tomato as a garnish. Simply slice the tomato and marinate it in a bit of the dressing that is being used. After the salad is prepared, tossed and ready to be served, gently lay the slices of tomato on top as a garnish. Voila! You have your tomato, and the salad is still crisp.

A word or two about the dressing: It should be prepared an hour or so in advance and chilled; then, after all the salad ingredients are blended together in that beautiful glass bowl, slowly add the dressing. Do NOT drown the salad. Lightly sprinkle a small portion of the dressing on the salad, and toss it gently until all the ingredients are evenly coated. Then TASTE it. Be objective! Is there enough dressing? Are the individual flavors distinct, subtle? If not, add a bit more, but remember: a salad should never have to do the breast stroke through the dressing to survive (unless you really like a soggy, limp salad!) Also note that an increasing number of really fine bottled dressings are available these days, so you may wish to save time by trying those alternatives. And, speaking of alternatives, if you do not wish to take the time to prepare greens yourself, there are some fine pre-packaged salad blends on the market.

GREEN BEAN VINAIGRETTE

1 teaspoon Dijon mustard	1 tablespoon herbed vinegar
3 tablespoons virgin olive oil	1 tablespoon lemon juice
1/4 cup water	1/8 teaspoon rosemary
1/2 teaspoon sugar	1/4 teaspoon freshly ground black pepper
1 1/2 pounds fresh green beans, rinsed and trimmed	
Water to steam	

Make vinaigrette by combining mustard, vinegar, oil, lemon juice, water, rosemary, sugar and pepper in a small bowl; refrigerate 1 hour. Meanwhile, steam green beans covered until just crisp tender—around 10 to 15 minutes; drain, chill and transfer to a serving platter. Drizzle with vinaigrette to taste. May be used as salad or in place of a hot veggie.
Yield: 6 servings.

INSALATA DE CAPRI

2 cucumbers, rinsed, tips removed, chilled, scored and sliced.
4 beds of watercress
1 cup light vinaigrette dressing
Salt to taste
Pepper to taste

> *Created in memory of the late Wallis Warfield, Duchess of Windsor, who was quoted as remarking: "A woman can never be too rich or too thin."*

With a fork, score the cucumbers lengthwise and slice; then place tender, chilled cucumber slices on beds of watercress and dress with a pale vinaigrette. Season with salt and pepper to taste. Serve with a peach tea (medium strong orange pekoe tea steeped in the traditional fashion, sweetened with 2 ounces of peach brandy, served in a tall glass over ice.)
Yield: 4 servings.

SPINACH SALAD WITH APPLES

12 ounces fresh baby spinach, pre-washed and trimmed
3 large red Delicious apples, cored and diced
8 ounces white button mushrooms, sliced
2 hard-cooked eggs, coarsely chopped
Salt to taste
Black pepper to taste
1 cup raspberry vinaigrette
1 cup garlic croutons
1/4 cup Asiago Cheese, grated

Prepare the salad in a large salad bowl just before serving. To the spinach, add the apples, mushrooms, eggs, salt and pepper; toss lightly to mix. Then, add the vinaigrette a bit at a time, tossing the salad to coat all the ingredients. Taste for preference, adding more dressing and salt and pepper as desired. Portion to individual chilled salad plates, top with croutons and cheese and serve.
Yield: 4 to 6 servings.

SPINACH SALAD à la NORMAND

1/4 cup wine vinegar
1/2 cup virgin olive oil
2 hard-cooked eggs, chopped
2 stalks celery, diced
Pepper to taste
2 cloves garlic, minced
12 ounces fresh baby spinach
1/2 cup onion, diced
Salt to taste

Prepare vinaigrette by blending vinegar, garlic and olive oil; set aside. In a salad bowl, toss spinach, eggs, onion and celery; drizzle vinaigrette over the salad and toss again until well coated. Season with salt and pepper to taste. Enjoy with warm French baguettes.
Yield: 4 servings.

SPINACH SALAD MANDARIN

1 pound fresh spinach, washed and drained
8 ounces fresh white button mushrooms, rinsed, drained and sliced
1 8-ounce can water chestnuts, drained and sliced
2 8-ounce cans Mandarin oranges (drain; reserve liquid)
1/2 cup virgin olive oil
2 tablespoons orange juice
2 tablespoons orange zest (grated rind)
1/2 cup reserved juice from Mandarin oranges
1 tablespoon vinegar
2 cloves garlic, minced
1/2 teaspoon freshly ground black pepper
1/2 teaspoon salt

Tear spinach leaves into a large salad bowl. Add mushrooms, water chestnuts and orange segments; lightly toss and chill for 10 minutes. In a small bowl, prepare vinaigrette dressing by combining oil, reserved Mandarin orange liquid, orange juice, zest, vinegar, garlic, pepper and salt; blend well. Drizzle vinaigrette dressing to taste over greens and toss.
Yield: 6 servings.

LEBANESE TABBOULEH SALAD

1 bunch scallions, finely chopped
1 1/2 cups fresh parsley, minced
1/4 cup fresh mint, minced
3 tomatoes, diced
2 cups boiling water, to soak wheat
1 cup cracked wheat, soaked and then drained of excess liquid
1/2 cup virgin olive oil
1/2 cup lemon juice
Salt to taste
Black pepper to taste
6 lettuce cups

This is a simple one. First, mix the wheat and water and cover; let stand at room temperature for about 2 hours. Squeeze out any excess liquid. Place scallions, parsley, mint, tomatoes and cracked wheat in a large bowl and toss gently until mixed well. Blend the oil and lemon juice well with a whisk. Drizzle on the wheat mixture and lightly toss to coat the ingredients. Add salt and pepper to taste and serve in the lettuce cups.
Yield: 6 servings.

CAESAR SALAD

1 head Romaine lettuce, washed and torn into bite-size pieces
2/3 cup virgin olive oil
1 clove garlic, finely minced
Salt to taste
Black pepper to taste
1/8 cup lemon juice
1 egg, beaten
6 to 8 anchovy filets, finely minced or whole (optional)
2 cups seasoned croutons
3/4 cup Pecorino cheese, grated

Place lettuce in a large salad bowl and toss as you sprinkle with the some of the oil (use just enough to coat the lettuce.) Add garlic and salt and pepper to taste; toss again. In a small bowl, whisk egg and lemon juice. Add egg mixture to lettuce and toss until thoroughly blended. Add the minced anchovies (if whole anchovies are used, place on top of prepared salad), croutons and half the cheese; toss again. Portion salad to chilled salad plates and top with remaining cheese.
Yield: 6 servings.

VEGETABLE SALAD

1 zucchini, diced
2 tomatoes, seeded and diced
4 stalks celery, diced
1 large Bermuda onion, diced
1/2 pound cauliflower florets, cooked just al dente, then chilled
1/2 pound broccoli florets, cooked just al dente, then chilled
2 cups green beans, cooked just al dente, then chilled
2 cups carrot sticks, cooked just al dente, then chilled
4 to 6 Romaine lettuce leaves
1 clove garlic, minced
2 to 4 cups balsamic vinaigrette dressing
Salt to taste
Black pepper to taste

In a large salad bowl, blend garlic and a bit of the dressing. Add the prepared vegetables, and begin to toss, adding more dressing, salt and pepper as needed to taste. Chill covered for about an hour. Spoon the salad onto lettuce leaves and serve.
Yield: 4 to 6 servings.

CHILLED SEAFOOD SALAD

3 firm tomatoes
1 to 2 cups oil and balsamic vinegar-style vinaigrette
12 ounces baby salad greens
1 to 1 1/2 pounds cooked fresh shellfish (try crab, shrimp, lobster, or a mix)
4 stalks celery, chopped
2 to 4 scallions, chopped
1 hard-cooked egg, chopped
Salt to taste
Black pepper to taste

Cut each tomato into 4 wedges, and drizzle with a bit of the dressing; chill. Just before service, toss the salad greens and well-chilled seafood to blend. Add celery, scallions and egg and toss again. Pour just enough vinaigrette to coat the salad (not drown it) and toss gently. Add salt and pepper to taste and toss again. Garnish with marinated tomato wedges.
Yield: 4 to 6 servings.

TUNA SALAD

1 8-ounce can albacore solid tuna, packed in spring water
1/4 onion, diced
4 tablespoons mayonnaise
Salt to taste
1/8 cup fresh parsley, finely chopped
1 tablespoon pickle relish, drained of liquid
Black pepper to taste

Drain the tuna well and flake into a mixing bowl. Add the onion, parsley, mayonnaise, relish, salt and pepper; gently toss to mix. Adjust mayonnaise and seasonings to taste. Chill well. Serve in fresh tomato cups, or as a sandwich on a toasted German rye bread, topped with Bibb lettuce, and a side of pickles.
Yield: 4 servings.

EGG SALAD

8 large hard-cooked eggs, cooled and chopped
1/4 small onion, diced
1/8 cup fresh parsley, finely chopped
4 tablespoons mayonnaise
2 tablespoons pickle relish, drained of most liquid
Salt to taste
Black pepper to taste

Put chopped eggs in a medium bowl; add onion, parsley, mayonnaise, relish, salt and pepper. Gently toss to mix thoroughly. Add more mayonnaise if desired; chill and serve with tuna salad or mixed green salad for a great summer meal, or as a sandwich for luncheon, on toasted farm bread with Butter lettuce, and pickles and chips.
Yield: 4 to 6 servings.

HAM SALAD

2 cups lean cooked ham, ground or minced
1/8 cup fresh parsley, finely chopped
1/4 onion, diced
Salt to taste
Black pepper to taste
1 tablespoons pickle relish
3 tablespoons mayonnaise
1 tablespoon Dijon mustard

Place ham, parsley, onion, salt and pepper in medium-size mixing bowl; toss to mix. Add relish, mayonnaise and mustard; mix well and chill. Wonderful served on rye toast with leaf lettuce, or as a salad scooped into fresh tomato cups. Yield: 4 servings.

VEGETABLE ANTIPASTO

2 large tomatoes, sliced thin
1 onion, shaved or sliced thin
1 bunch fresh parsley
1/2 cup balsamic vinegar
1 1/2 cups virgin olive oil
Salt to taste
Black pepper to taste
1/8 teaspoon garlic powder
1 cup celery, diced
2 14-ounce cans small whole cooked white potatoes, drained and diced
1 pound snow pea pods, cooked and chilled
2 cups cooked broccoli florets, cut into bite-size pieces and chilled
2 large hard-cooked eggs, crumbled

Arrange tomatoes, onions and fresh parsley sprigs around the edge of a chilled platter; set aside. In a large mixing bowl, combine the vinegar, oil, salt, pepper, and garlic powder; whisk until well blended. Add celery, potatoes, pea pods and broccoli and gently toss to coat well. Drain of excess dressing and transfer to center of serving platter; top with crumbled egg. Yield: 6 servings.

✓ HELPFUL HINTS - (Stuff your grandma should have told you!)

- Buying in bulk saves lots of money.
- If slippery items slide as you're cutting them, dip your fingers in salt.
- Plastic wrap is great until it comes time to use it, and then the only thing it will stick to is itself. Secret: Keep it cold in the fridge.
- Burned your fingers? Run them under very cold water and then dab them with a paste made from baking soda and water. (Ah, relief!)
- A fire on the back burner or in the oven? Douse quickly with salt or baking soda. (Of course, if the fire is climbing the walls, it's definitely time to call 911!)
- Does the meatloaf or meatball mix stick to your hands during preparation? Keep rinsing your hands in cold water and they'll become a non-stick surface.

VEGETABLES: garden delights

"Doubt who you will but never yourself."
—Christian Bovee

The mention of vegetables elicits a variety of reactions: from the turned-up noses of junior and sis, to the meat-and-potato attitude of Dad, to Mom's "Well, it's convenient" attitude toward a can of peas.

I recall that as a child I was never too thrilled at the prospect of having to face anything on my plate that even remotely resembled a carrot, green bean, or (God forbid) a mushroom. The all-too-familiar exhortation of "Eat your vegetables, they're good for you" didn't seem to faze me in the least.

Mothers command us to just TRY something, and while we secretly might WANT to try it, it's the fact that it's Mom doing the requesting that makes us rebel. Unfortunately, these attitudes can, and usually do, follow us into adulthood and are passed on to the next generation, in what seems to be a never-ending cycle. The cycle can be broken, however, by inviting ourselves and the kids to experience new taste thrills, new awareness of nutrients, new health.

The wonders that can be brought to the table and the palate via cauliflower, zucchini, broccoli, mushrooms, and the like are really awesome—flavors, heavenly aromas and untold nutrients that are too often lost or ignored in preparation.

Think about this: When confronted with the frenzy of modern living and the "flash" of canned, frozen and convenience foods, how often do you buy FRESH? How many restaurants really serve FRESH? Are "convenience" foods (TV dinners, canned foods, packaged and frozen) REALLY that convenient? When all is said and done, we frequently go through the motions—the routine of eating—without really considering what marvelous machines our bodies are, or how to properly protect and care for them. The average modern body probably consumes more additives, junk foods, detrimental substances and fillers than REAL food, and is in a constant state of rebellion (headaches, indigestion, backache, nausea, sluggishness and nervousness).

We can take a step toward combatting these demons, with fresh, tasty, nutritious vegetables. When thinking about vegetables, the following rule is prime: Use fresh always, if available; use frozen only when fresh is not available; and never use canned (well, almost never).

With vegetables, you are limited only by your imagination and your willingness to explore and experiment. So, let's do just that. We'll start with the basics, give you some background, alternatives and suggestions, and explore a few myths along the way. And then, it's up to you! So, on with the apron gentlemen, and away we go. (Coming along, ladies?)

In the vegetable world, perhaps one of the more maligned, yet popular residents is the venerable carrot, introduced to America by the British. There is a myth that persists to this day, that we must purchase carrots with their bright green tops securely attached. According to the legend, this means they're "really fresh." And, of course, we must peel them to within a millimeter of their very existence, to get rid of that "unhealthy and dirty skin." The next insult is that we cut them into the tiniest, bite-sized pieces as a convenience to our jaws. The final coup de grace is that we proceed to boil them in heavily salted water until "tender" (too often a euphemism for "mush"), then drain off the liquid, add more salt, (with maybe a touch of pepper and butter), and then serve "it."

In reality, what have we done?
1) We've not purchased wisely.
2) We've not prepared wisely.
3) We've not served wisely.

What we have done is to lose most, if not all, of the nutritional value and ingest what is, in essence a "filler" for which our bodies cannot be entirely grateful. After all, a carrot is a carrot, right? WRONG!

When purchasing carrots, buy the very freshest—those uniform in size, bright orange in color, not bruised, not wilted, decayed or otherwise damaged. Tops should NOT be attached (this will minimize loss of moisture and nutrients). The best carrot is smaller and bright orange, available year-round, and is rich in vitamin A, iron, niacin, riboflavin and thiamine, while remaining low in calories. Carrots should be refrigerated as soon as possible after harvest and remain refrigerated until prepared. To retain freshness in storage, try sprinkling them with water, wrapping them in paper toweling or cloth, and storing them in the vegetable crisper drawer of the fridge.

Some basic rules for all vegetables are:
- Keep them under refrigeration and avoid exposure to the air.
- Peel and trim them very carefully to avoid waste and loss of nutrients.
- Peel fresh veggies just before cooking.
- Cook veggies whole or in their skins wherever possible to retain nutrients.
- Avoid stirring cooking veggies – the agitation increases the loss of color and nutrients.

As for preparation, try steaming. Do not peel carrots; simply remove the tops and bottom tips, and brush them lightly under cool water with a vegetable brush. This will guarantee maximum retention of vitamins and nutrients in the skin and body. Ideally, carrots should be cooked whole but for generally acceptable aesthetics and handling, they may be cut into pieces. Just remember, the smaller the pieces, the greater loss of nutrients in cooking. (Try slicing them after preparation and just prior to presentation.)

By far, steaming and stir-frying are the best ways to cook almost any vegetable. If you try steaming as an alternative to boiling, you'll need a collapsible steam basket (they're really inexpensive and available in most supermarkets and discount stores). Place just enough water in the bottom of a pot or pan large enough to accommodate the basket. Water level should be just to the bottom of the basket, but not high enough to touch the vegetables when inserted. Bring the water to a boil, insert the filled basket, close the lid, and steam for 7 to 10 minutes, depending on the degree of doneness desired. Before you cook them to death, try this: LESS TIME. You may be surprised at wonderful results you didn't expect, flavors and textures you had forgotten, and maximum nutrient value. It's so simple; why not give it a try?

As wonderful as steamed carrots may be, (or any veggie, for that matter) , they might rapidly become a bit boring, if there were not so many ways to dress them up. Some recipes follow, with many variations, but I still encourage you to experiment (albeit carefully) with spices, herbs and seasonings. Remember, the idea is to enhance or complement the natural flavors—not to mask them.

CARROTS VICHY

1 pound fresh carrots, trimmed and cleaned
Water to steam
1 tablespoon unsalted butter, margarine or corn oil
1/2 cup almonds, slivered
1/2 cup orange juice, fresh or frozen (with pulp)
1/4 cup dark brown sugar   1/2 cup raisins
Black pepper to taste   Parsley to taste
Dash of salt (optional)

Steam carrots for 7 minutes, as you simultaneously measure and prepare the other ingredients. Heat butter, margarine or oil in a large frying pan over medium-low heat, so that it doesn't burn; add almonds and sauté until lightly browned; add orange juice and simmer. Add brown sugar, raisins, pepper, parsley and salt, stirring constantly until slightly syrupy. Remove from the heat and add carrots, folding them into the prepared sauce to blend well; serve. *(You'll get rave reviews on this one.)*
Yield: 4 to 6 servings.

CARROT MEDLEY

1 pound fresh carrots, cleaned and trimmed
Water to steam   2 tablespoons unsalted butter, margarine or corn oil
1 small onion, diced   1/2 small green bell pepper, diced
1/4 pound fresh white button mushrooms, sliced
Pinch of salt   Pinch of black pepper
Pinch of ground ginger

Steam carrots for 7 minutes, as you simultaneously measure and prepare the other ingredients. Heat butter, margarine or oil in a large frying pan over medium-low heat to prevent burning; add the onion and green pepper and sauté gently until onion is glassy (about 5 to 7 minutes). Add the mushrooms and stir-fry for 1 or 2 minutes. Season with salt, pepper and ginger (go easy on the ginger) to taste. Fold carrots into the mixture until well blended; serve.
Yield: 4 to 6 servings.

HERBED LEMON ASPARAGUS

1 pound fresh green asparagus spears, cleaned and trimmed
Water to steam   4 tablespoons butter
1/4 teaspoon sweet basil   Dash oregano
2 tablespoons fresh lemon juice

Steam asparagus for approximately 15 minutes; asparagus should be crisply done and tender but not overcooked. While asparagus is cooking, heat butter, basil, oregano and lemon juice in a skillet. When the asparagus has finished steaming, remove the spears to a serving platter and top with the sauce just before serving.
A very elegant accompaniment to any meal.
Yield: 2 to 4 servings.

CAULIFLOWER GRATINEE

1 medium cauliflower, cut into small florets
Water to steam
1/2 cup (1 stick) butter
2 tablespoons all-purpose flour
2 1/2 cups milk, scalded
Heavy pinch nutmeg
Salt to taste
Black pepper to taste
3 tablespoons Parmesan cheese, grated
Non-stick cooking spray
1/2 cup breadcrumbs

Rinse cauliflower florets in cold water. Steam the florets in a medium saucepan until just tender (a bit more than al dente) about 5 to 7 minutes. Test for doneness. In another saucepan, over low heat melt 1/4 cup of the butter; whisk in flour. Add milk, nutmeg, salt, pepper and cheese; stir constantly and continue to cook over low heat until very smooth. Remove from heat. Then, arrange the florets in a shallow, oven-proof dish sprayed with cooking spray and totally cover them with the cheese sauce, sprinkle with the bread crumbs, and dot with the remaining 1/4 cup of butter. Place under the broiler until browned. Even those who hate cauliflower will like this one.
Yield: 4 to 6 servings.

GREEN BEANS LEBANON

2 pounds fresh green beans, cleaned and trimmed
Water to steam
3 cloves garlic, minced
1 medium onion, finely chopped
1/2 cup virgin olive oil
1/2 teaspoon dry mint
Salt to taste
Black pepper to taste
1/4 teaspoon ground allspice
2 medium tomatoes, chopped

Steam green beans covered for about 7 to 10 minutes until just al dente. Sauté onion and garlic in olive oil in a large fry skillet until tender. Add mint, salt, pepper, allspice and chopped tomato and continue sautéing until thoroughly heated. Gently fold in the beans and heat through.
Yield: 6 servings

BAKED BROCCOLI

1 pound broccoli, cleaned and cut into small florets
Water to steam
Non-stick cooking spray
1/2 cup milk or cream
Salt to taste
Black pepper to taste
1 14-ounce can cream of mushroom soup
1 14-ounce can French-fried onions

Steam broccoli florets covered for 5 to 7 minutes until just al dente. While broccoli is cooking, preheat the oven to 350 degrees and spray a baking dish with cooking spray. Combine the milk or cream, salt, pepper and soup; mix well. When broccoli is cooked, layer half of the florets in the baking dish, and cover with half the soup mixture, then top with half the onions. Layer the rest of the broccoli on top of the onions and cover with the balance of the soup mixture. Bake 25 to 30 minutes, topping with the remaining onions for the last 5 minutes.

Yield: 6 servings.

GREEN POLE BEANS WITH WATER CHESTNUTS

2 pounds fresh green pole beans, cleaned and ends trimmed
Water to steam
1/2 cup (1 stick) butter
1 small onion, finely chopped
1 8-ounce can water chestnuts, drained and sliced
1/4 teaspoon ground ginger
Salt to taste
Black pepper to taste
1/2 tablespoon soy sauce

Steam whole green beans until done crisply (about 10 minutes). While they're cooking, melt the butter and sauté the onions and water chestnuts with the ginger, salt, pepper and soy sauce in a small sauté pan until heated through. Place the cooked beans in a serving dish and top with the butter sauce.

Yield: 6 servings.

GREEN PEAS à la FRANÇAISE

1 8-ounce package frozen green peas
2 sprigs fresh parsley, chopped
1/2 cup (1 stick) butter, melted
Black pepper to taste
3/4 cup water

1 16-ounce jar baby onions, drained
6 iceberg lettuce leaves, shredded
Salt to taste
1 teaspoon sugar

In medium saucepan, combine frozen peas with baby onions, parsley, shredded lettuce, 1/4 cup melted butter, salt, pepper and sugar; toss well and set aside, refrigerated, for an hour. After an hour, add water, cover and bring to an easy boil; quickly reduce heat and simmer (barely bubble) for about 15 minutes or until the liquid is almost totally reduced. Remove pan from the heat, add remaining 1/4 cup butter and gently fold or toss (don't stir) until veggies are coated. *This is a different way to serve peas, especially to those jaded souls who grimace when they see peas on the menu.*
Yield: 4 to 6 servings.

CREAMED BABY SPINACH

1/2 cup (1 stick) butter, softened
9 ounces baby spinach leaves, rinsed and drained slightly
Salt to taste · Black pepper to taste
Pinch sugar · Pinch nutmeg
1/3 cup heavy cream · 1 teaspoon all-purpose flour

In a large sauté pan, melt the butter and add the rinsed spinach with just the water it has retained from rinsing. Cook covered over medium-low heat, stirring occasionally for about 3 to 5 minutes or until spinach is just limp. Remove pan from the heat and toss spinach with salt, pepper, sugar and nutmeg, mixing well. In a small bowl, blend the cream and flour with a whisk. Return spinach to the stove and continue to cook for just a few moments. Add the remaining butter, stir in the cream and flour mixture and, while stirring constantly, simmer until creamy.
Yield: 4 servings.

BAKED ACORN SQUASH

2 1-pound acorn squash
4 tablespoons orange marmalade
Black pepper to taste

4 tablespoons butter
Salt to taste
Cinnamon to taste

Preheat oven to 375 degrees. Cut each squash in half lengthwise and remove seeds. Place 1 tablespoon butter and 1 tablespoon marmalade in center of each squash half. Season with salt, pepper and cinnamon. Tightly wrap each squash half in a large section of heavy aluminum foil; place squash on baking sheet cut-side up, and bake for 45 to 60 minutes or until tender.
Yield: 4 servings.

SNOW PEA PODS

2 cups boiling water
1 pound snow pea pods, rinsed with tips and any strings removed
2 tablespoons butter
1 cup sour cream
Heavy dash nutmeg
Salt to taste
Black pepper to taste
1 8-ounce can water chestnuts, drained and sliced

Boil water in a medium saucepan; add snow peas. When the water returns to full boil, cook covered no longer than 2 to 3 minutes or until just crisp tender. Remove from heat, drain and set aside in a warm serving dish. Melt the butter in the sauce pan; add the sour cream, nutmeg, salt, pepper and water chestnuts. Sauté over low heat until heated through. Pour cream sauce over the snow peas.
Yield: 4 servings.

SAUTEED SKILLET MUSHROOMS

4 tablespoons butter	1 tablespoon onion, minced
1 clove garlic, minced	8 ounces whole white baby mushrooms
Salt to taste	Black pepper to taste
Splash dry white wine	1/4 cup Asiago cheese, grated

Heat butter in a large sauté pan; add the onion and garlic and sauté until the onion is glassy and the garlic golden. Add the mushrooms, salt and pepper and sauté briskly over medium high heat for about 3 or 4 minutes, remembering to toss and stir to keep from burning. Add the splash of wine and toss while cooking another few moments until hot. Transfer to serving platter and sprinkle with cheese.
Yield: 4 servings.

BRUSSELS SPROUTS MOUTARD

4 tablespoons cornstarch	1/2 cup cold water
1 pound baby Brussels sprouts	1 14-ounce can vegetable broth
3 tablespoons lemon juice	2 tablespoons Dijon mustard

Blend the cornstarch and water in a small bowl and set aside. In a medium saucepan, cook the sprouts in the broth over medium-high heat until just crisply tender, about 15 to 20 minutes. Remove from the heat. Strain and remove sprouts (reserving broth) and hold in a warm, covered dish. Return the broth to the heat, adding the lemon juice and mustard, and returning to a semi-boil. Then add the cornstarch mix, stirring until thickened to desired consistency. Pour sauce over the warm sprouts.
Yield: 4 to 6 servings.

GREEN BEANS ASIAGO

1 pound fresh green beans, washed and trimmed
Water to steam   1/2 cup virgin olive oil
Salt to taste   Black pepper to taste
1 clove garlic, minced   1/4 teaspoon rosemary
1/4 teaspoon sweet basil   1/2 cup Asiago cheese, grated

Steam beans for about 10 to 15 minutes until crisply tender. Remove beans to a covered warm serving dish. In a separate bowl, mix olive oil, salt, pepper, garlic, rosemary and sweet basil. Drizzle the mixture over the beans to coat them completely. Serve topped with cheese.
Yield: 4 servings.

POTATO DAUPHINOIS

Non-stick cooking spray
6 medium Russet potatoes, peeled, rinsed and thinly sliced
1/2 cup Asiago cheese, grated (or another grated cheese)
1 cup milk, scalded   1 cup heavy cream
1 egg, beaten   Heavy pinch nutmeg
Salt to taste   Black pepper to taste
1/2 cup (1 stick) butter

Preheat oven to 400 degrees. Spray a 2-by-9-by-13 baking pan or dish with cooking spray. In a large bowl, mix potatoes, cheese, milk, cream, egg, nutmeg, salt, pepper and half the butter; pour into the baking dish. Top with dots of remaining butter and bake 50 to 60 minutes, until potatoes are tender and top is browned.
Yield: 4 to 6 servings.

WHOLE PARSLEY POTATOES

1 tablespoon virgin olive oil   1 onion, diced
2 cloves garlic, minced   Salt to taste
1/2 teaspoon black pepper   1 14-ounce can chicken or beef stock
1/2 cup fresh parsley, chopped
2 14-ounce cans whole small white potatoes, drained
(Or 16 ounces small whole frozen potatoes)

Heat oil in a large skillet or fry pan over medium heat; add the onion, garlic, salt and pepper and sauté for several minutes until tender. Add the broth and 1/4 cup of the parsley; blend while bringing to a boil. Add the potatoes (uncrowded) and return to a boil; reduce heat to simmer covered until some of the liquid has reduced, an additional 10 minutes or so, until heated through. Remove potatoes to a serving dish; top with some of the sauce from the skillet and remaining fresh parsley.
Yield: 4 to 6 servings.

LYONNAISE POTATOES

2 pounds whole Russet potatoes, peeled	Water for boiling potatoes
1/2 cup (1 stick) butter	Salt to taste
Black pepper to taste	2 onions, thin sliced
1 small clove garlic, minced	1 tablespoon fresh parsley, chopped

Boil potatoes for 5 to 10 minutes, or until just slightly undercooked; drain, chill and slice. Heat 1/4 cup of the butter in a large skillet. Add potatoes, salt and pepper, and cook over medium heat for another 10 minutes until potatoes are cooked (gently toss potatoes while cooking to prevent sticking). Heat the remaining 1/4 cup butter in a separate small fry pan, and cook the onions and garlic just until a bit browned. Add onions and garlic to the potatoes. Continue to cook another few minutes, gently tossing frequently. Serve sprinkled with parsley.

Yield: 4 to 6 servings.

BAKED POTATOES

4 medium to large Idaho baking potatoes
2 tablespoons cooking oil (Optional)   1/2 cup fresh chives, chopped
Butter, low-fat sour cream or shredded cheese of choice, as topping for potatoes.
Salt to taste   Black pepper to taste

Preheat oven to 425 degrees. Clean potatoes with vegetable brush (brush lightly!) under cool water; dry. If you like a softer skin, rub potatoes with oil and place on middle rack of oven. If you don't rub the skins with oil, they'll brown and crisp (to many this is the best part).Cook approximately 1 hour until thoroughly cooked (to test, jab with a fork.) To serve, slit each potato down the middle, compressing the inner pulp; add chives, butter, and/or low-fat sour cream or cheese, and salt and pepper according to your tastes.

Yield: 4 servings.

GARLIC MASHED POTATOES

6 medium Russet potatoes, peeled and quartered

Water to cover	2 tablespoons virgin olive oil
2 cloves garlic, finely minced	4 tablespoons butter
2 tablespoons sour cream	Up to 1/4 cup warm milk
Salt to taste	Black pepper to taste

Add enough cold water to cover potatoes in a large saucepan and bring to a boil, then reduce heat to simmer 15 to 20 minutes or until potatoes are tender. While potatoes are cooking, place olive oil and garlic in a small skillet and cook over low heat for a few minutes until garlic is pale, stirring occasionally. Drain the potatoes and place in a mixing bowl; add butter and garlic–oil mixture and mash with a potato masher. Add the sour cream and mix; then slowly add in just enough warm milk to obtain desired consistency. Add salt and pepper, and whip the potatoes. Goes great with a meatloaf.

Yield: 4 to 6 servings.

BAKED BEANS

2 pounds dried White Northern beans, sorted and rinsed
2 large onions, diced
2 pounds smoked ham hocks
Equal parts water and tomato juice to cover beans
Additional water as needed
1/2 to 3/4 pound dark brown sugar
1 cup tomato catsup

Soak sorted beans in just enough cold water to cover; let sit for about 6 hours. In a large crock pot (or preferably a cast-iron kettle) combine drained beans, one half the diced onion, the ham hocks, tomato juice and water to cover. Bring to a boil and reduce to simmer covered until beans are cooked according to package directions (but not mushy) about 3 hours; you may have to add a small amount of additional water while cooking, but most of the liquid should cook off. When beans are tender, remove ham hocks and set aside to cool; remove meat from ham bones and fold the meat gently into the beans. Fold brown sugar, remaining onion and catsup into the bean-ham mixture. Bake uncovered in a preheated 350-degree oven for 1 1/2 to 2 hours. Serve piping hot with corn bread.

Yield: 6 to 8 servings.

DR PEPPER BAKED BEANS

1 28-ounce can pork and beans
Non-stick cooking spray
1 medium onion, diced
1/2 green bell pepper, finely chopped
1 medium tomato, finely diced
1/2 cup dark brown sugar
1/3 cup Dr Pepper soft drink
1/8 teaspoon ground cloves

Preheat the oven to 350 degrees and spray a casserole with non-stick cooking spray. Drain liquid from the pork and beans; pour the beans into the baking dish, gently mixing in the onion, green pepper and tomato. In a small bowl, combine brown sugar, Dr Pepper and ground cloves until sugar is dissolved. Pour liquid evenly over the beans, and bake uncovered for 30 minutes.

Yield: 4 to 6 servings.

✓ ■■■■■■■■■■■■■■■■■■
HELPFUL HINTS - (Stuff your grandma should have told you!)

- Are you being called "garlic" or "onion fingers" because of the fragrance on your hands? Rinse them in cold water and drag out the good old baking soda again (salt also will work here) and rub it into your hands; then rinse in cold water. POOF, like magic, the nasty fragrance is gone.

- Stained fingers and hands? The juice of a lemon rubbed over the offending area performs magic. You can use a slice of raw potato the same way.

- To keep potatoes from "budding" place an apple in the bag.

- If you accidentally over-salt something being prepared with a lot of fluid, drop in a peeled potato while cooking and it'll absorb much of the excess salt. In less liquidy dishes, add a touch of vinegar and sugar.

- To soften hardened brown sugar, place a slice of apple in with it.

■■■■■■■■■■■■■

PASTA & RICE
carbo heaven

"Most people's thoughts are someone else's opinions."
—Oscar Wilde

With the myriad of pasta types available, you'll want to be aware of the best combinations with various sauces. From the very hearty to the delicate, not every sauce and pasta are compatible. Knowing some basic combinations will help ensure your pasta dishes are perfect every time. These are merely guidelines; the ultimate choice of which pasta to use is yours. When cooking pasta, "al dente" is the rule; overcooking will turn pasta to mush, and in turn ruin a great pasta dish. Also, to keep the water from boiling over when cooking pasta, rub the inside of the pot with a bit of oil.

PASTA TYPES

PASTA TYPES:	COMBINATIONS:
Small Bow ties, shells, and corkscrews	*Best served with tomato and meat sauces, oil-based and cheese sauces.*
Large Lasagna, fettuccine, and ravioli	*Hearty enough for substantial meat sauces, cheeses, etc.*
Regular Spaghetti, linguine	*Best with lighter sauces like marinara or al olio.*
Very Thin Spaghettini, capellini vermicelli, and angel hair	*Best used with extremely light sauces or soups.*
Straw pasta Bucatini and perciatelli	*A great pasta for heavy cream or cheese sauces.*
Tubes Rigatoni, ziti, elbows, etc.	*This hearty pasta is the greatest for heavy, chunky tomato and meat sauces.*
Delicate Orzo, pastina, etc.	*While many enjoy these with a bit of butter, salt, pepper and Asiago cheese, they are primarily for use in soups.*

A brief mention of rice now: As bread is to America, rice is to the Far East. There are many types, but basically they are either long or short grain. The long grain is usually more acceptable in most recipes as it stays separated, whereas the short grain tends to become softer. When cooking rice, be aware that the volume of rice will triple if not quadruple during cooking, so use an appropriate-sized pan. When cooking, add a few drops of oil to the water to keep the rice separated. Do not stir the rice if possible during cooking as this tends to mush it; if you must fluff it, do so gently using a fork. There are so many ways to prepare rice—from saffron to almonds—so here's where your imagination can come into play.

RAVIOLI AMATRICIANA

1/2 pound salt pork, rind trimmed, pork diced
1/4 pound bacon
1 medium onion, minced
1 clove garlic, minced
2 29-ounce cans Italian-style tomatoes, peeled - not drained
1/2 teaspoon dry red pepper flakes (optional)
3 dozen small to medium frozen ravioli (meat or cheese filled)
Grated Parmesan cheese to taste
Salt to taste
Black pepper to taste

In a large skillet, cook salt pork and bacon over medium heat until bacon is crisp; remove the pork and bacon, drain and set aside. Sauté the garlic and onion in bacon/pork drippings for about 10 minutes or until golden. Mash the tomatoes (or use kitchen-ready). Add tomatoes, pork, crumbled bacon and red pepper flakes (optional) to garlic-onion mixture. Simmer uncovered for 30 minutes, stirring occasionally. Cook the ravioli according to package directions, so the finish times of pasta and sauce coincide. Drain the ravioli, and transfer to individual serving dishes; top with the sauce, and sprinkle with cheese, and salt and pepper as desired.
Yield: 4 to 6 servings.

CAPELLINI AND CHICKEN

1 1/2 tablespoons virgin olive oil (additional as needed)
1 small onion, diced
2 chicken breasts (1 to 1 1/2 pounds, skinless and cubed)
1 large raw carrot, diced   1 small green pepper, diced
1/2 to 3/4 pound broccoli florets   2 cloves garlic, minced (or to taste)
1 12-ounce package capellini (angel hair pasta)
1 cup chicken broth   1 teaspoon dry sweet basil
3/4 cup Asiago cheese, grated

In a large frying pan or skillet, heat one tablespoon of olive oil. Add half the onion and cubed chicken, cooking over medium-high heat for about 5 minutes or until chicken is cooked through. Remove chicken to paper toweling to drain oil. In a large pot, start the water for the pasta to boil. Add the other 1/2 tablespoon of olive oil to skillet; add the carrot, remaining onion, garlic, green pepper, and broccoli, cooking by stir-frying for about 5 or 6 minutes until tender, adding additional oil as needed. Place the pasta in the boiling water to cook (remember: "al dente"). Add the chicken broth to skillet along with the basil and just a dash of the cheese; combine. Add cooked chicken back into the skillet; reduce heat to simmer covered for an additional 5 minutes until pasta is ready. Drain the pasta but do not rinse. Place on serving dishes, topped with the chicken-vegetable topping. Use the remaining Asiago cheese to sprinkle on top of each serving.
Yield: 4 to 6 servings.

FUSILLI CARBONARA

1/2 pound bacon
1 pound fusilli pasta
1 clove garlic, minced
4 large eggs, beaten
1 cup heavy cream (or sour cream)
Salt to taste
Black pepper to taste
1/2 cup Parmesan cheese, grated

Cook bacon in heavy skillet until crisp. Remove bacon from pan and drain on paper towels; crumble bacon when cool. Cook the fusilli al dente in a large pot of water per package directions. When about 5 minutes of cooking time remains, sauté the garlic in a bit of the bacon drippings left in the skillet; cook about 2 minutes or until golden. In a bowl, mix together eggs, cream (or sour cream), salt and pepper and pour into the skillet. Cook until mixture just begins to reach a creamy consistency; remove from the heat. Pasta should now be done; drain it quickly but do not rinse. In a large bowl, toss pasta with sauce until coated; add crumbled bacon and toss again. Portion into individual pasta dishes and top with cheese.
Yield: 4 servings.

FETTUCCINE ALFREDO

1 pound fettuccine pasta
1 cup butter, melted
1 to 2 cloves garlic, minced
1 cup heavy cream, heated
2 cups Asiago cheese, grated
Salt to taste
Black pepper to taste

Prepare fettuccine al dente according to package directions. While pasta is cooking, sauté the garlic in butter for a few minutes in a small skillet. When pasta is done, drain quickly but do not rinse. In a large bowl, toss the pasta with the garlic butter, cream, 1 cup of the cheese, salt and pepper. Portion into individual pasta dishes and top as desired with remaining 1 cup of cheese. A bit high in calories, but, oh, so good!
Yield: 4 servings.

TURKEY TETRAZZINI

4 tablespoons butter
1 clove garlic, minced
1 medium onion, chopped
1/2 pound fresh white button mushrooms, cleaned and sliced
1/4 cup all-purpose flour
3 1/2 cups milk or heavy cream
1/2 teaspoon salt
1 teaspoon black pepper
2 tablespoons cooking sherry
3 cups cooked turkey, cut into bite-sized pieces
1 8-ounce can water chestnuts, sliced and drained
1 12-ounce package capellini or thin spaghetti
Non-stick cooking spray
1/2 cup Parmesan cheese, grated
Dash of paprika

Preheat oven to 350 degrees. Melt 1 tablespoon butter in a large skillet or sauté pan. Sauté the onion, garlic and mushrooms until tender, about 4 or 5 minutes; remove from the pan and set aside. Melt the remaining butter in the same pan; blend in flour until smooth, whisking for 2 or 3 minutes, being careful not to brown flour mixture. Continue as you whisk in milk or cream and season with salt and pepper, cooking until slightly thickened. Add the reserved mushroom mixture, sherry, turkey and water chestnuts. Simmer just until warmed through, and remove from heat. Cook the pasta in a large pot of boiling water until almost al dente (about 3 to 4 minutes). Drain and rinse in cold water to stop cooking. Spray a 2-quart casserole dish with non-stick cooking spray. Spread half the pasta evenly across the bottom of the dish, mix in a bit of the sauce, and top with the remaining pasta and sauce mixture. Sprinkle with the grated Parmesan cheese and a light dusting of paprika. Bake uncovered for 30 minutes or until heated through. Great served with a spinach salad and warm farmhouse bread.
Yield: 6 servings.

CAPELLINI ISABELLA

4 tablespoons virgin olive oil
3 cloves garlic, minced
3 fresh tomatoes, seeded and cut into chunks
Salt to taste
1 pound capellini pasta
1/2 cup Asiago cheese, grated

1/2 onion, minced
8 ounces fresh white button mushrooms, sliced

Black pepper to taste
1 pound zucchini, cubed with ends trimmed
1/2 cup dry white wine

Bring water to a boil for the pasta. Heat olive oil in a large sauté pan or skillet over medium heat; add the onion and garlic, sautéing until onion is glassy and garlic is just golden. Add the mushrooms, tomatoes, salt and pepper and continue cooking covered another 3 to 4 minutes. Prepare the pasta according to package directions, cooking about 3 to 4 minutes until al dente. While pasta is cooking, add the zucchini to the sauce along with the wine and 1/4 cup of the Asiago cheese. Gently stir sauce until zucchini is lightly cooked, about another 3 to 4 minutes; remove from heat. Pasta should now be ready; drain the pasta but do not rinse. Move pasta to a large bowl, top with some of the sauce and gently toss until mixed. Serve hot on individual plates, topped with more sauce and the remaining 1/4 cup of Asiago cheese. Terrific served with warm Italian bread and a salad.
Yield: 4 servings.

LINGUINE & CLAM SAUCE

1 tablespoon virgin olive oil
3 cloves garlic, minced (or to taste)
1/2 teaspoon oregano
1 cup dry red wine such as Cabernet Sauvignon (more as needed)
2 dozen fresh clams (in the shell)
1 29-ounce can kitchen-ready tomatoes (already diced)
1 tablespoon fresh parsley, chopped

1 medium onion, minced
1 bay leaf
1/2 teaspoon basil

1 pound linguine pasta

1/2 cup Parmesan cheese, grated

Heat a large pot of water for the linguine. Heat oil in a large skillet over medium heat. Add the onion and garlic, cooking until onion is glassy and garlic is golden; add the bay leaf, oregano, basil and wine and quickly bring mixture to a boil. Add clams and additional wine as needed and cover, cooking about 5 minutes over medium-low heat or until the clams open. Transfer clams to a heated bowl and discard any that haven't opened. Add the linguine to the boiling water, cooking according to package directions until al dente; drain well. While pasta is cooking, add the tomatoes to the skillet with the chopped parsley; top with the clams and continue to cook for 5 minutes; remove the bay leaf. Set aside the clams and about half of the sauce. Add the cooked pasta to the remaining sauce in a large bowl and toss to thoroughly mix. Serve in individual heated pasta bowls, surrounded by the clams, topped with a bit more sauce, and grated cheese.
Yield: 4 servings.

PERCIATELLI à la PESTO

3 cloves garlic
1/2 cup pine nuts
1 3/4 cups fresh basil leaves
1 cup baby spinach leaves, rinsed
1 cup + 2 tablespoons virgin olive oil
3/4 cup Pecorino cheese, grated
1 pound perciatelli pasta

To prepare the sauce, place the garlic, pine nuts, basil, spinach and 3/4 cup of the olive oil in a blender or food processor; "pulse" puree. The puree tends to thicken, so remember to scrape down the sides of the container and mix it a few times. Transfer the basil mixture into a bowl and whisk in 1/4 cup of oil a bit at a time, making sure to blend well on each addition. Add 3/8 cup of cheese to the basil mixture and blend well. Let the sauce set at room temperature for about an hour, then simmer in a small saucepan over very low heat while pasta is being prepared. (It's really easy to make the sauce, but if you'd rather save some time, there are several home-style prepared pesto sauces available.) Boil water in a large pot for the pasta. Add one tablespoon of olive oil to the water and cook pasta according to package directions until al dente. When pasta is done, drain quickly but do not rinse. Return pasta to the pot, adding the remaining 2 tablespoons of olive oil, and tossing to coat the pasta. Add less than half the pesto sauce and continue tossing to coat. Portion pasta into individual pasta bowls. Top with remaining pesto sauce and grated cheese.
Yield: 4 servings.

ZITI ROMANO

1/2 cup butter
1/2 pound ricotta cheese
1 pound ziti pasta
Salt to taste

1 clove garlic, minced
2 cups heavy cream
1/2 cup Romano cheese, grated
Black pepper to taste

Melt 1/4 cup butter in a large skillet and sauté the garlic until golden; turn heat to very low. Add ricotta cheese, cream and remaining 1/4 cup of butter; simmer uncovered for five minutes, stirring occasionally. Remove from heat and cover. Meanwhile, cook pasta according to package directions. When finished, drain quickly but do not rinse. In a large bowl, toss the pasta with the sauce until well coated. Portion into individual pasta dishes, top with the Romano cheese and season with salt and pepper to taste. In spite of the ingredients, not as caloric as it sounds, about 700+ per serving.
Yield: 4 servings.

VERMICELLI WITH SAUSAGE & MEATBALLS

Sauce

1 29-ounce can crushed Italian-style tomatoes

2 29-ounce cans tomato sauce   2 bay leaves

1 6-ounce can tomato paste, blended with 6 ounces cold water

Salt to taste   Black pepper to taste

1 cup water (use as needed)   1 cup red wine (optional)

1/2 onion, minced   2 cloves garlic, minced

1 tablespoon sugar   1 tablespoon sweet basil

1/2 pound white baby mushrooms, sliced

Meatballs

1 1/2 pounds ground sirloin   1 small onion, minced

2 cloves garlic, minced   1/2 cup Italian-style breadcrumbs

Touch of oregano or Italian seasoning blend

1/4 cup Parmesan cheese, grated   Salt to taste

Black pepper to taste   1 egg, beaten

1 tablespoon Worcestershire sauce   1/4 cup tomato catsup

1 to 2 cups virgin olive oil for sautéing

1 pound sweet or hot Italian sausage links

1 pound vermicelli pasta

In a large saucepan, combine all the sauce ingredients over very low heat and simmer covered an hour or two, stirring occasionally. (The longer it cooks, the better it becomes—all day over very low simmer would be great.) Be sure to correct the liquid as the sauce cooks, adding a bit more water or wine as needed.

Once the sauce has started, prepare the meatballs as follows: In a large mixing bowl, crumble up the ground sirloin. Add the onion, garlic, breadcrumbs, just a TOUCH of oregano (it's powerful!), cheese, salt and pepper. Toss until mixed together; add beaten egg, Worcestershire sauce and catsup. Mix well until blended but don't mash it together too tightly because that tends to toughen the meatballs. If the meat mixture is still too loose or "soupy" add more breadcrumbs to the mix until the meat holds a ball shape when formed. Heat 1 cup of the oil in a large skillet over medium heat. Cut each sausage link into quarters; brown them on all sides in the skillet, drain and add them to the sauce. Then, using your hands, roll the beef into an even number of meatballs (about 8 to 12), cooking a few at a time in the skillet until browned, continuously rolling them in the oil so they don't burn. (Sticky hands? Rinse in cold water frequently.) Remove browned meatballs and drain on paper towels; then add them to the sauce for the remainder of the cooking period. (Remember: the longer, the better).

When dinnertime rolls around, prepare the vermicelli according to package directions until al dente. When done, drain pasta and return to the pot. Add a tablespoon of the olive oil to the pasta and toss; then add 1/2 cup or more of the sauce to your preference and toss. Portion pasta into individual pasta bowls, top with meatballs and sausage, additional sauce and grated cheese. A green salad! Italian bread! The pasta! *What more could you want?*

Yield: 4 to 6 servings.

ZITI PRIMAVERA

1 29-ounce can diced tomatoes, Italian-style	
2 6-ounce cans tomato paste	Water to blend paste
3/4 cup fresh broccoli florets	3/4 cup carrots, thinly sliced
3/4 cup onion, thinly sliced	1/2 cup red wine
3/4 cup zucchini, diced into bite-sized pieces	
1 red bell pepper, julienne sliced	3 cloves garlic, minced
2 bay leaf, whole	1 tablespoon olive oil
1/4 teaspoon oregano	1/4 teaspoon thyme
1/2 teaspoon rosemary	1/2 teaspoon sweet basil
1 teaspoon salt	1/2 teaspoon black pepper
1 teaspoon granulated sugar	1 pound ziti

Blend the tomato paste and water and combine with all the other ingredients in a large pot; blend well and bring to a boil. Reduce to simmer covered about 1 hour until all the veggies are tender. Serve over prepared ziti and top with grated cheese.

Yield: 4 to 6 servings.

FETTUCCINE ALFREDO WITH CHICKEN

1 pound fettuccine	1/2 pound butter
1 clove garlic, minced	1 pound broccoli florets, pre-blanched
1 zucchini, ends trimmed and diced	
1 1/2 pounds chicken breast, pre-cooked and diced	
Salt to taste	Black pepper to taste
1/2 pint sour cream	1/2 pint heavy cream
1/2 cup Asiago cheese, grated	1/2 cup Pecorino cheese, grated

Cook pasta according to package directions until al dente. While pasta is cooking, sauté the garlic in butter in a large sauté pan over medium heat. Add broccoli florets, raw zucchini and cooked chicken to the garlic mixture and sauté until the veggies are "al dente." When pasta is ready, quickly drain, but do not rinse; return pasta to the pot. Add the sauce, season with salt and pepper to taste and toss to coat the pasta. Blend the sour cream and heavy cream in a separate bowl and add to the pasta, continuing to gently blend and toss. Reduce the heat to simmer and add three-quarters of each type of cheese, continuing to toss until well coated and blended. When heated through, portion onto individual pasta dishes and top with remaining grated cheeses. Serve with a Caesar salad. Did somebody say this was low fat? Guess not, but the word is *"Yum!"*

Yield: 4 to 6 servings.

AMERICAN CHOP SUEY

1 pound elbow macaroni
2 cloves garlic, minced
2 tablespoons virgin olive oil
1 29-ounce can chopped tomatoes
Black pepper to taste

1 onion, diced
1 red pepper, seeded and diced
1 to 1 1/2 pounds ground sirloin
Salt to taste
Grated Parmesan cheese to taste

Bring water to a boil in a large pot and cook macaroni according to package directions until just "al dente." While pasta is cooking, sauté the onion, garlic and red pepper in olive oil in a large skillet over medium heat, until onion is glassy and garlic golden; add the ground beef and sauté until cooked through. Drain excess fat from meat mixture and add the tomatoes, adjusting the seasoning as required. Reduce heat to medium-low and continue cooking covered until thoroughly heated. Drain the macaroni, but do not rinse, and return macaroni to the pot. Add the beef mixture to the pasta and toss to completely mix. Serve in pasta bowls topped with cheese.
A great New England classic.
Yield: 4 to 6 servings.

BAKED MACARONI & CHEESE

1 pound elbow macaroni
2 cups milk
3 tablespoons all-purpose flour
2 tablespoons butter
1/8 teaspoon ground nutmeg
Salt to taste
Black pepper to taste
3 cups extra sharp cheddar cheese, (regular or low fat)
Non-stick cooking spray
1/4 cup Parmesan cheese, grated

Preheat the oven to 350 degrees. Cook the macaroni in a large pot of water according to package directions until almost al dente; rinse, drain and set aside. While pasta is cooking, pour 1 1/2 cups of the milk into a medium saucepan. In a small bowl, whisk together the flour with the remaining 1/2 cup milk until smooth. Warm the milk in the sauce pan, and whisk in the milk/flour mix, cooking over medium-low heat until thickened, smooth and bubbly. Reduce heat to simmer. Stir in the butter, nutmeg, salt, pepper and cheddar. Continue cooking while stirring for another 2 minutes until cheese is melted, and then remove from heat. Add the cheese sauce to the pasta and mix to thoroughly combine. Coat a deep baking dish with non-stick cooking spray. Pour macaroni into dish and sprinkle with Parmesan cheese; bake uncovered 30 minutes or until golden brown and bubbly.
Yield: 4 to 6 servings.

ITALIAN STUFFED SHELLS

1 pound lean ground beef or ground chuck

1 medium onion, chopped	2 cloves garlic, minced
1 8-ounce can beef bouillon	1/2 cup fresh parsley, chopped
1 tablespoon fresh basil, chopped	Black pepper to taste

1 1/3 cup Parmesan cheese, grated

1 12-ounce package jumbo macaroni shells

1 26-ounce jar of your preferred pasta sauce

2 cups Mozzarella cheese, shredded

Prepare shells according to package directions until just al dente. Drain and rinse, and cool. Preheat oven to 350 degrees. Sauté the ground beef, onion and garlic over medium heat in a large skillet until cooked; drain excess fat. Add the bouillon, parsley, basil, pepper and 1/3 cup of Parmesan cheese and mix well. Cook until most of the liquid is reduced and remove from heat. Lightly grease a large, shallow baking dish (about 2 inches-by-9 inches-by-13 inches). Stuff each of the shells with the beef mixture, and place in the dish, cover with the pasta sauce, and top with the Mozzarella cheese and remaining Parmesan cheese. Bake covered for 30 minutes, and uncovered another 5 minutes. Enjoy with an Italian salad and bread.

Yield: 4 to 6 servings.

RICE PILAF

3 cups low-salt chicken broth

1 1/2 cups brown or white uncooked rice

8 ounces fresh white button mushrooms, cleaned and sliced

1 carrot, trimmed and coarsely grated

1/4 teaspoon marjoram

1/4 teaspoon celery seed

1/4 cup onion, shaved

2 tablespoons fresh parsley, chopped

Bring chicken broth to a boil in a large saucepan. Add the rice, mushrooms, carrot, marjoram, celery seed and shaved onion. Cover and reduce heat to just barely simmer for about 25 minutes until rice is tender and until all liquid is absorbed. Mix well and transfer to a serving bowl; top with chopped parsley.

Yield: 4 servings.

SPANISH RICE

1 tablespoon virgin olive oil
1 tablespoon garlic, minced
1 small onion, finely chopped
2 cups chicken or vegetable consommé
1/2 teaspoon ground cumin
1/2 teaspoon chili powder
1 small red bell pepper, seeded and minced
1 medium green pepper, diced
2 cups quick-cooking white rice
1 large tomato, seeded and diced
1 1/2 cup Jack cheese, shredded

Heat oil in a large sauté pan over medium heat. Add the garlic and onion and cook for 3 to 5 minutes. Add the broth, cumin, chili powder and diced pepper; mix and bring to a boil. Remove from the heat, add the rice and cover for 5 to 10 minutes until all liquid is gone. When prepared, add tomato and cheese and serve. Yield: 4 servings.

ARMENIAN STYLE RICE

10 tablespoons butter
1 cup uncooked egg noodles, extra fine
2 cups long-grain raw white rice
4 cups water, boiling
Salt to taste
1/2 cup fresh mint, minced (or to taste)

This great recipe comes from a dear Armenian friend, and is absolutely wonderful when served with shish kabobs.

Heat 6 tablespoons butter in a large skillet over medium-high heat. Add the noodles and quick-fry them until golden brown (about 3 to 4 minutes). Next, add the raw rice and continue stir frying another five minutes until the rice is golden. Now, add the water and salt to taste. Stir, cover and boil gently over medium heat until all liquid is gone, which should take about 20 minutes. In a small saucepan, melt the remaining 4 tablespoons of butter, add the mint and heat until just warm. When rice is ready to serve, gently fold the mint-butter into the rice.
Yield: 4 to 6 servings.

MUSHROOM RICE

2 cups regular white rice
4 cups water
4 tablespoon butter
Salt to taste
2 tablespoons onion, minced
1/2 teaspoon garlic, minced (or to taste)
1/4 pound fresh white button mushrooms, sliced

In a medium large saucepan, combine rice, water, 1 tablespoon butter, salt, onion and garlic. Bring to a boil. Then reduce heat and simmer covered until all liquid is absorbed, according to rice package directions. In a separate small saucepan, sauté the mushrooms in the remaining 3 tablespoons butter for 3 to 5 minutes; remove and keep warm. When rice is finished, fold mushrooms gently into the rice and serve.
Yield: 4 servings.

RISOTTO AMANDINE

2 cups regular white rice
4 tablespoons butter
1/2 teaspoon almond paste or almond extract
1 cup blanched almonds, slivered

4 cups water
Salt to taste

1/2 cup raisins

In a medium-large saucepan, combine rice, water, 1 tablespoon butter, salt and almond paste or extract. Bring to a boil. Then reduce heat and simmer covered until all liquid is absorbed, according to rice package directions. In a separate small saucepan, sauté the almonds and raisins in the 3 tablespoons butter for about 3 or 4 minutes until the almonds are browned. When rice is prepared, gently fold the almond-raisin mixture into the rice and serve.
Yield: 4 servings.

GARLIC TOAST

1/4 cup virgin olive oil
4 tablespoons minced garlic
12 slices Italian bread

No Italian meal would be complete without garlic bread. It's easy to prepare and it's great for dipping into sauce, so none gets lost.

Preheat the oven to 400 degrees. Mix together the oil and garlic. Place the bread slices on a baking sheet and brush with the garlic mix. Bake for 15 minutes until the bread is golden brown. Move to a covered bread basket to keep warm for serving.
Yield: 6 to 12 servings.

☑ **HELPFUL HINTS** - (Stuff your grandma should have told you!)

- Have you used too much sugar? Add a few drops of lemon juice.
- To determine if an egg is fresh, immerse it in a pan of cool, salted water. If it sinks, it's fresh. If it swims to the surface, get rid of it.
- Stains from tomato-based sauces on the plastic containers? Spray the containers with non-stick cooking spray first. "Voilà!" No more stains.
- Eggshells crack while hard-cooking? Be sure eggs are at room temperature before boiling. Add a splash of vinegar or a pinch of salt to the water; no more cracks.
- You say you have leftover wine? Don't throw it out; freeze it into ice cubes for future cooking use.
- Stuff a marshmallow in the bottom of an ice cream cone to stop those messy drips.

MEATS:
on the hoof

"Grub first - then ethics."
—Bertolt Brecht

There are so many varieties and variations on a theme that a complete volume might be devoted to meats; however, that is not our intention. This chapter is simply a working introduction and includes some popular recipes to try.

BEEF

It seems that the American diet revolves around meats of one type or another and the "leader of the pack" is BEEF. Many beef cuts tend to be a bit expensive, but it finds its way to the table nonetheless.

There are several methods of cooking beef:

ROASTING or DRY HEAT

This cooking method seems to be the most popular and is also a great choice for preparing other meats—like pork or lamb. Cooking slowly in a moderate oven (about 325 degrees) may take a bit longer, but will produce flavorful, evenly cooked, delicious roasts, with a minimal amount of shrinkage. Meat should always be placed on a rack—fat side up—in a roasting pan, to cook to desired doneness; a meat thermometer inserted into the center of the roast (not touching the bone) is an ideal cooking aide, letting you know when the roast is done to perfection. No guesswork!

BRAISING or MOIST HEAT

Using this method, the meat is browned in a skillet or sauté pan, then covered and simmered slowly with a bit of liquid until tender. This can also be done in a low oven from 275 to 300 degrees and is usually the preferred method to use for pot roasts and meats that are only minimally tender.

STEWING or LIQUID COOKING

This method is used for the least tender cuts of meat, and for cooking items like pork shoulders or corned beef. Meats should be covered with a liquid such as stock, wine or water and set to simmer covered until tender. This can be achieved either in the oven or on top of the range.

PAN FRYING or SAUTEING

In this method, meats are cooked in a bit of fat, butter or oil over moderate heat, uncovered until nicely browned, and cooked to degree of desired doneness.

BROILING

This cooking method requires meats to be cooked under a direct gas flame or electric coil at a distance of 3 to 5 inches. This is a particularly nice method for steaks and chops. Meat should be placed on a broiler rack and browned first on one side, turned and browned on the other to seal in the juices, and then continue to cook to desired degree of doneness.

CHARCOAL GRILLING

This preparation method is great for the outdoor enthusiast, but it will take a bit longer to cook the meat than if you sautéed or broiled it.

BEEF ROAST CHART

(Times are approximate)

ROAST/ WEIGHT	TIME PER LB./TEMP.	INTERNAL TEMP.
Standing Rib 5-8 pounds	20 min. @ 300° - Rare	120 to 130°
	25 min. @ 300° - Medium	150 to 160°
	30 min. @ 300° - Well done	160 to 170°
Sirloin 8-10 pounds	20 min. @ 300° - Rare	120 to 130°
	25 min. @ 300° - Medium	150 to 160°
	30 min. @ 300° - Well done	160 to 170°
Standing Rump 5-8 pounds	25 min. @ 300° - Rare	120 to 130°
	30 min. @ 300° - Medium	150 to 160°
	35 min. @ 300° - Well	160 to 170°
Top Round 3-5 pounds	30 min. @ 300° - Rare	120 to 130°
	35 min. @ 300° - Medium	150 to 160°
	45 min. @ 300° - Well done	160 to 170°
Eye of Round /Rib Eye 3-5 pounds	8 to 10 min. @ 350° - Rare	120 to 130°
	12 to 15 min. @ 350° - Medium	150 to 160°
	18 to 20 min. @ 350° - Well done	160 to 170°

PEPPERED BEEF ROAST

3-pound eye round roast or tenderloin roast
2 cloves garlic, minced
1 small onion, minced
1/4 cup virgin olive oil
1/2 teaspoon rosemary
1/2 teaspoon thyme
1 tablespoon fresh black pepper, coarsely ground
1/2 teaspoon oregano

Preheat the oven to 500 degrees. Insert meat thermometer into the thickest section of the roast. Mix garlic and onion into the oil and paint it onto the meat roast using a pastry brush. Next, mix the rosemary, thyme, black pepper and oregano and sift onto the roast to cover. Place the roast on a rack in a baking pan and bake for 15 minutes. Reduce the heat to 350 degrees and continue baking for an additional 30 minutes or until meat thermometer reads 140 to 145 degrees for medium rare, 150 to 160 degrees for medium doneness, and for the rare enthusiasts, it should read about 120 to 130 degrees. *Something for everybody.*
Yield: 6 servings.

TERIYAKI KABOBS

1 pound top round steak, cubed
4 tablespoons soy sauce
1/4 teaspoon ginger
1 cup pineapple chunks
12 (or more) cherry tomatoes
3 tablespoon honey
1/2 cup pineapple juice
1 clove garlic, minced
1 green bell pepper, cubed

A great item for the outdoor grill: this recipe takes a minimal amount of time in preparation before cooking.

In a baking dish, cover the steak cubes with a marinade of honey, soy sauce, ginger, pineapple juice and garlic (or use your favorite marinade). Cover and marinate in the refrigerator for about 15 minutes. Then skewer the steak cubes, alternating with pineapple chunks, peppers and tomatoes. Grill for about 5 minutes on each side (or to your desired degree of doneness), basting with the balance of the marinade, discarding any that is leftover. Great with a special salad and a rice pilaf.
Yield: 4 servings

UNCLE FATTY'S MEATLOAF

2 pounds ground beef (85 percent to 95 percent lean)
1/2 cup onion, finely chopped
1/2 cup fresh white button mushrooms, chopped
2 eggs, well beaten
1/2 cup Italian breadcrumbs
2 to 3 cloves garlic, minced
1/2 cup catsup + additional for topping
1/2 cup Parmesan cheese, grated + additional for topping
Dash cinnamon (Just a SPRINKLING – a little goes a long way!)
Dash salt
Black pepper to taste

Preheat oven to 350 degrees. Combine all ingredients in a large mixing bowl (first make sure that you spread the drop cloths to cover the kitchen). Use a light tossing motion to mix, adding more crumbs and catsup if needed, until mix molds into a loaf that holds together nicely (mashing it tends to toughen the end product). Form into a loaf in a lightly greased or non-stick loaf pan or dish; top with additional catsup and sprinkle with additional Parmesan cheese. Bake for about 45 minutes to an hour; remove and let stand 5 minutes before slicing. *Enjoy! (Perhaps with whipped potatoes, mushroom gravy and fresh broccoli hollandaise?)*
Yield: 6 servings.

POT ROAST OF BEEF

3-pound rump roast or bottom round roast
1 cooking bag with spices
2 cups tomato juice
1/4 cup red wine
2 tablespoons wine vinegar
3 potatoes, peeled and cut in quarters
10 carrots, cleaned, trimmed and halved
2 onions, thinly sliced
1/2 bunch celery stalks with their leaves, cleaned, trimmed and halved
1 green bell pepper, cored and chopped
2 cloves garlic, minced

Preheat the oven to 325 degrees. Pierce the roast with a fork in several places on both sides. Prepare cooking bag spices with juice, wine and vinegar instead of water. Place roast into bag (following bag instructions) in large roasting pan, arranging vegetables inside the bag, around and over meat and covering with prepared liquid; tie bag with bag ties, cutting slits in the top of the bag to vent steam. Place roast in oven and roast according to bag directions, until very tender. Remove meat carefully from bag (remember the steam) and let set to firm up for a few minutes. Place on platter and slice, arranging vegetables around the beef. Reserve gravy to top meat.
A simple "one-bag" meal; no muss, no fuss, not a lot of pans to wash.
Yield: 6 to 8 servings.

POT ROAST OF BEEF &
BROWNED POTATO à la FRANÇAIS CANADIEN

4- to 5-pound chuck roast
Black pepper to taste
Non-stick cooking spray
6 to 8 potatoes, peeled and chunked
Salt to taste
1 small onion, thinly sliced
3 cups water

Preheat oven to 325 degrees. Put the roast, which has been rubbed with salt and pepper and topped with the sliced onion, on a rack in a heavy roasting pan (preferably an old-fashion cast iron one) sprayed with cooking spray. Add 1 cup of the water; cover and cook for 2 hours. Add another cup of water and cook for 1 more hour. Add remaining water and potatoes around the beef and cook for an additional 1/2 hour.
Yield: 8 to 10 servings.

NEW ENGLAND POT ROAST VARIATION

5 pounds veal bones   Water to cover veal bones
1 6-ounce can tomato paste   6 ounces water to mix paste
32 ounces cranberry juice   5-pound pot roast
1/4 cup virgin olive oil   3 cloves garlic, whole
1 tablespoon all-purpose flour per each cup liquid

This takes a while to prepare, but is delicious.

First, make a stock by browning veal bones in a 350-degree oven for one hour or until bones are browned. Place bones in a large soup pot, add water to cover, and simmer over low heat for 3 to 4 hours. Strain the veal stock and discard the bones. Add the tomato paste mixed with water and cranberry juice to the stock, blend well and simmer over lowest heat covered again for 2 to 3 hours. Check frequently and add more water as needed. In a large covered oven-proof skillet, brown the roast on all sides in the olive oil; Add garlic and veal stock to cover. Cover the pot and put in a 325-degree oven for about 2 hours or until tender. Remove pot roast to a warm platter, cover and let set for about 10 minutes for ease in slicing. To make gravy, slowly whisk appropriate amount of flour into the remaining liquid until desired consistency is reached. Slice and serve with whipped potatoes and your choice of vegetables.
Yield: 10 to 12 servings.

STEAK AU POIVRE (Peppered Steak)

1/2 cup butter
1 clove garlic, minced
2 tablespoons Worcestershire sauce
1 small onion, minced
1/4 cup fresh parsley, finely chopped
1/4 teaspoon Dijon mustard
2 tablespoons black pepper, coarsely ground
4 8-ounce New York-cut sirloins

Combine butter, garlic, Worcestershire sauce, onion, parsley, mustard and 1 tablespoon of the pepper in a small saucepan over low heat until butter is melted. Brush the steaks on both sides with the mixture (reserving balance), dust with the remaining pepper, and place steaks under the broiler. Broil to your preference. Serve steaks topped with remaining heated butter pepper mixture, and perhaps a baked potato with sour cream and chives, and fresh steamed asparagus.
Yield: 4 servings.

BEEF BOURGUIGNON

3 pounds top round or chuck
1 to 2 bay leaves, whole
2 cups red wine
1/2 teaspoon black pepper
Thyme to taste
4 tablespoons butter
2 tablespoons quick-mix flour
1/2 pound salt pork, diced
1 14-ounce jar pearl onions, drained
8 ounces whole white button mushrooms

1 small onion, sliced
2 tablespoons virgin olive oil
1/4 teaspoon salt
Parsley to taste
1 clove garlic, minced
2 cups water
1 14-ounce can beef consommé
1 carrot, cleaned, trimmed and sliced

This dish is one of the most famous dishes on the tables of France, and while it sounds "très chic," it is simple to prepare, delicious, and one that will have the guests clamoring for more. A little tip is to prepare it ahead of time, refrigerate it, and reheat for later use. It can also be frozen. Ready? Let's go!

Using a deep bowl or dish, combine beef (either whole to be sliced later, or cut into large cubes (cubed meat seems to infuse the flavors much better—and you don't have to think of slicing) and marinate. Create marinade by blending the sliced onion, bay leaf, oil, wine, salt, pepper, parsley, thyme and garlic. Cover the meat with the marinade, refrigerate and turn it somewhat frequently, for about an hour. After marinating, remove the meat to a platter, strain the marinade and set the liquid aside. Meanwhile, heat 2 tablespoons butter in a large covered skillet or heavy sauté pan and add the meat (again, preferably cubed) until browned evenly on all sides; set the meat aside. Blend the water and flour and add to the consommé in the same skillet, stirring constantly for 3 or 4 minutes; stir in the reserved, strained marinade, bringing to a boil and then lower to simmer. Return the meat to the skillet, cover and simmer for about 1 3/4 to 2 hours or until meat is tender. Once this part of the cooking process has started, in a separate medium sauté pan, add the salt pork, 2 tablespoons butter, carrots and pearl onions, and sauté over medium heat for 10 to 15 minutes. Add this mixture (minus the salt pork and drained of excess fat) and the button mushrooms to the covered skillet. Continue to simmer covered for another 15 minutes or until done. *Voilà—you'll have the tastiest meal imaginable.* Great served with a side of buttered noodles or whole parsleyed baby potatoes.
Yield: 6 to 8 servings.

BRAISED BISTRO BRISKET

5 pounds lean beef brisket	1 bunch celery
6 to 8 carrots	5 to 6 small onions
Non-stick cooking spray	3 tablespoons virgin olive oil
Garlic, minced (to taste)	Catsup to cover meat
2 to 3 bottles beer of your choice, or enough to just cover roast	

Preheat oven to 350 degrees. While oven is heating, clean and quarter onions and clean and cut celery and carrots into large chunks. Rinse the meat and pat dry with paper toweling. In a large, covered roasting pan that has been sprayed with cooking spray, sear the meat on all sides in the oil, and remove from roaster. Then place the vegetables and garlic in the bottom of the roaster, and place the meat on top, fat side up. Pour the beer over the meat, so that it's just slightly covered and not totally submerged; cover the top of the meat with the catsup. Cover roasting pan tightly and cook for 3 hours without removing cover. Then, remove the cover and continue cooking for another 1/2 hour, adding a bit more beer if too much liquid has evaporated. Remove brisket from the roaster and let set for 5 minutes before slicing thinly across the grain. Serve with the vegetables and top with the oven juices if preferred.

Yield: 10 to 12 servings.

GREEN PEPPER STEAK ORIENTAL

3/4 cup soy sauce
1/2 teaspoon ground ginger
1 clove garlic, minced
1 pound round steak, sliced into thin strips against grain
1/2 cup virgin olive oil
1 1/2 cups water
1 green pepper, cored and cut into strips
3 stalks celery, chopped
1 cup scallions, chopped
1 tablespoon cornstarch
2 tomatoes, cubed

Add the soy sauce, ginger and garlic to the beef strips and toss together. Next, heat the oil in a large skillet over high heat. Remove the meat from the marinade, add to the sauté pan and stir-fry, tossing until browned; add 1 cup water and reserved marinade, cover and reduce heat to simmer for 20 to 30 minutes or until tender; Add the green peppers, celery and scallions and additional water if needed; simmer about 10 minutes longer or until vegetables are tender. In a small bowl, mix the cornstarch and 1/2 cup water until blended and add to the mix, stirring and cooking until sauce is slightly thickened. Add the tomatoes to heat through; serve. Great with a fried rice dish.

Yield: 4 servings.

ROAST BEEFSTEAK SANDWICH

2 tablespoons butter
1 large onion, shaved or sliced thin
Salt to taste
Black pepper to taste
1 to 11/2 pounds roast beef, shaved (rare, medium or well)
6 large crusty French rolls, pocket-cut, heated
12 slices cheese of your choice, thin sliced

Melt butter in a large skillet and sauté the onions with salt and pepper until glassy; remove onions from the pan and keep warm. Place meat in the skillet and heat through. Fill the warmed rolls with the meat, onions and slices of cheese. *Enjoy! Great for a fast lunch.*
Yield: 6 servings.

BEEF ENCHILADAS DE MEXICO

6 tablespoons virgin olive oil
1 pound fresh ground sirloin or ground round
1 8-ounce can tomato sauce
1/2 cup onion, chopped
1/2 cup green bell pepper, cored and chopped
1 14-ounce can kidney beans, drained
8 soft flour tortillas
Non-stick cooking spray
1/2 pound Jalapeño cheese, shredded
1/2 cup fresh tomato, chopped

Preheat oven to 350 degrees. Heat 2 tablespoons of the oil in a large skillet and brown meat over medium-high heat; drain any excess fat. Add tomato sauce, onion and peppers, cooking and stirring for about 5 minutes over medium heat. Add the beans and continue to cook for a few minutes; remove from heat. In a separate large fry pan, dip the tortillas in the rest of the heated oil for a few moments; then drain on paper toweling. Spoon an equal amount of half of the meat mixture onto each of the tortillas and roll them up. Spray a shallow 2-by-9-by-13-inch roasting pan with cooking spray, and place the rolled tortillas seam down and side by side in the pan. Top with the remaining meat mixture, and bake covered for 15 minutes. Top with cheese and fresh tomatoes and continue baking uncovered another 5 minutes until cheese is melted. Great with Mexican-style rice.
Yield: 4 servings.

SICILIAN-STYLE STUFFED STEAK ROLLS

14 ounces fresh baby spinach, rinsed and roughly shredded
7 tablespoons virgin olive oil
1 onion, diced
3 cloves garlic, minced
2 pounds round steak (in single large slices, 1/2 inch thick or thinner)
1/4 cup Pecorino cheese, grated
1/4 cup Italian breadcrumbs
1/4 pound ground pork
1/4 cup fresh parsley, chopped
Salt to taste
Black pepper to taste
1 large raw egg, beaten
3 large eggs, hard-cooked, sliced or crumbled
1 pound total of equal amounts of Italian cold cuts (such as salami and prosciutto)
AND cheese (provolone or gorgonzola), all diced or cut into julienne strips
1/2 cup fresh or frozen peas
2 to 3 ounces pork fat, finely diced
2 cups dry red wine (plus more as needed during cooking)
2 cups beef broth
2 tablespoons tomato paste
2 tablespoons water to blend paste

> *This dish is not one you will be making every day, but it IS superb for that special occasion, or when you want to expand your taste buds with a bit of the "grand cuisine" of Italy. Sure, it takes a bit of time, but don't be frustrated. Approach it with love, and it won't disappoint you. All set to go?*

Preheat oven to 350 degrees. To begin, wash the spinach well in cold water and drain; place the spinach in a large pot with just the residual water from the rinse, and cook over medium heat gently for a few minutes until tender. Remove the spinach and let it cool; then drain and squeeze out as much of the liquid as possible and set spinach aside.

Now, heat half the olive oil in a large skillet, adding the onion and garlic and sautéing until golden; remove from the heat and place in a large mixing bowl and set aside. Pound the steak(s) to 1/4-inch thickness or so, being careful not to tear the steak. In the large mixing bowl, mix the Pecorino cheese, the breadcrumbs, the ground pork and the parsley in the large bowl with the onion and the garlic. Add salt and pepper to taste; at this point, add the beaten raw egg, and gently blend the mixture adding more breadcrumbs as needed. Now, spread the mixture evenly on the steak(s); then spread the hard-cooked eggs the length of the steak(s). Scatter the diced or julienned cold cuts, cheeses, peas, spinach and the pork fat evenly on top. (*Yes, I suppose it DOES look like the beginning of a*

"Dagwood" sandwich, but we're almost done, so hang in there).

Now comes the tricky part; tightly but gently roll the steak(s) over the stuffing mixture so it doesn't ooze out the ends. It should resemble a log. Tie it in several places with white cooking twine, to secure it during cooking. Now, carefully brown the meat roll in a heavy skillet in the remaining olive oil, turning it often until browned. Then, place steak(s) in a lightly greased oven-proof casserole dish. In a small saucepan blend wine, broth and tomato paste blend and bring to a boil; pour wine mixture over steak(s). Immediately, put covered casserole dish in the oven for 2 hours until meat is tender, basting the meat often, and checking for sufficient liquid, adding more wine as necessary. Remove from the oven, and let the meat set up for about 10 minutes. Skim any fat residue from the remaining liquid and hold liquid to use as a sauce. Prior to serving, cut the strings and slice. Bravo! You have just made a winning Italian dish that tastes great with a pasta and salad.

Yield: 6 to 8 servings.

WILD BILL'S CHILI

2 medium Vidalia (or standard yellow or white) onions, coarsely chopped
1/2 green bell pepper, chopped
3 cloves garlic (or more to taste), minced
1/8 cup olive oil
1 pound ground sirloin
1 bay leaf, crushed
1/4 teaspoon oregano
1/8 cup chili powder
1 27-ounce can red kidney beans, undrained
1 teaspoon salt
1 tablespoon vinegar
1/4 teaspoon red hot chili peppers, crushed (or to taste)
1 14-ounce can crushed tomatoes
1/2 cup shredded cheddar and Monterey jack cheeses

> *This is not too spicy, so vary the amount of "heat" according to your taste. It definitely is NOT the 12-alarm chili Texas is noted for, but one more suitable for American tastes in general. Cousin Bill really likes this one and prepares it often. If he can make this, so can you.*

In a larger, heavy kettle, sauté the onion, green pepper and garlic in the oil over medium heat, until onions are golden (about 8 to 10 minutes) remembering to stir occasionally. Add the ground sirloin, bay leaf and oregano and continue to sauté while loosening the bulk size of the meat, and cook until meat is cooked through. Add the chili powder, beans, salt, vinegar, chili peppers and tomatoes and blend together; reduce heat to barely simmer uncovered for 1 1/4 to 1 1/2 hours, while stirring occasionally. Serve topped with shredded cheese. I personally like this served with a side of white rice and a salad.

Yield: 6 servings.

BEEF STROGANOFF

6 tablespoons butter	1 onion, diced
8 ounces whole white baby mushrooms	
1 1/2 to 2 pounds tenderloin of beef, cut into 1/2 inch strips	
Salt to taste	Black pepper to taste
1 1/2 tablespoons all-purpose flour	2 1/2 cups beef consommé
1 teaspoon Dijon mustard	2 pints sour cream

While beef stroganoff traditionally has just a "bit" of sour cream and no mushrooms, we have come to know it a bit differently. Here's our variation (oh, sacrilege).

Heat 3 tablespoons of butter in a large skillet over low heat; when melted add onion, mushrooms, beef strips, salt and pepper. Stir-fry until onion is glassy and the meat fairly well cooked; remove from heat. In a separate skillet or larger soup pot, melt the remaining 3 tablespoons of butter and blend in the flour until smooth. Whisk consommé into the butter mixture and heat, whisking continuously until thickened a bit, about 5 minutes. Whisk in the mustard. Then add the sour cream and stir over moderately low heat until heated through. Lastly, add the beef, onion and mushroom mixture, and continue heating over low heat until very hot. Serve over wide egg noodles. While it may break with "tradition," we hope you'll agree it's a winner. Yield: 4 to 6 servings.

LAMB

"Mary had a little lamb, its fleece was white as snow, and everywhere that Mary went, the lamb was sure to go..."

Many cooks seem to fear and misunderstand the preparation of this wonderful meat. For years, we believed (and many still do) that it must be prepared extremely well done, when in fact cooking it until just pink and juicy is the ideal. Then of course, we have to get past seeing those cute little sheep that we occasionally count as we drift off to sleep.

These cute little guys come to us at different ages:

Baby lamb	about 6 weeks old
Spring lamb	about 4 months old
Plain old lamb	6 months to a year old

When purchasing lamb, remember that the older the lamb, usually the tougher the meat. Always think of youth being synonymous with tender, and purchase accordingly.

LAMB ROAST CHART

(Times are approximate.)

ROAST/WEIGHT	TIME PER LB./TEMP. ALL MEDIUM DONENESS	INTERNAL TEMP.
Whole Leg, 5-10 pounds	20 min. @ 350°	160 to 170°
Leg Sirloin, 5 pounds	20 min. @ 325°	150 to 160°
Rib/Rack Roast, 2-3 pounds	15 to 20 min. @ 350°	150 to 160°
Crown Roast, 5-8 pounds	15 to 20 min. @ 375°	150 to 160°

RACK OF LAMB

2 pound lamb rack (about 8 ribs)
1/2 cup breadcrumbs
2 cloves garlic, minced (or to taste)
1/2 teaspoon dry thyme
1/4 teaspoon black pepper
4 tablespoons Dijon or spicy brown mustard

Preheat the oven to 350 degrees. Trim all fat from lamb. In a small bowl, combine breadcrumbs, minced garlic, thyme, pepper and mustard. When thoroughly blended, rub over the lamb to coat. Place on rack in baking pan in oven and cook to desired amount of doneness (see chart), 45 to 60 minutes. Remove from oven and let set for about 5 minutes. Slice and serve with mint jelly and rice pilaf.
Yield: 4 servings.

LOIN OF LAMB

2 pound loin of lamb
2 tablespoons lemon juice
2 cloves garlic, 1 minced and 1 slivered
1/2 teaspoon oregano
1/2 teaspoon thyme
1/2 teaspoon rosemary
1/2 teaspoon black pepper

Start with loin of lamb that has been trimmed, boned and tied. In a small bowl, combine lemon juice, minced garlic (amount according to your taste), oregano, thyme, rosemary and pepper. Rub the mixture over the lamb to coat. Then stab several slits into the fat side of the lamb loin and insert slivers of garlic into the slits; cover lightly and refrigerate 4 to 5 hours; then place in a pre-heated 325-degree oven for 25 to 30 minutes per pound or until done to your preference. If using a meat thermometer, it should read 145 degrees when done juicy pink. Let set for a few minutes before slicing. Perhaps serve with Green Beans Lebanon and baked potatoes.
Yield: 4 servings.

TRADITIONAL HERBED LEG OF LAMB

1 5-pound leg of lamb
1/3 cup vinegar
1 tablespoon fresh crushed mint
1 tablespoon crushed rosemary
1 tablespoon thyme
2 cloves garlic (1 minced, 1 slivered)
1 teaspoon salt
1/2 teaspoon fresh black pepper, coarsely ground

Preheat oven to 325 degrees. Place lamb fat side up on a rack in roast pan and pierce several times with a knife or fork; insert slivers of garlic. In a small bowl, combine all other ingredients and rub the mixture over the lamb to generously coat. Roast uncovered for about 1 1/2 hours, or until meat thermometer reads 150 degrees when inserted into thickest part of the meat for medium doneness (internal temperature should read 160 degrees for more well done meat). Remove from oven and let stand to firm up before slicing. Accent with orange-mint marmalade.
Yield: 8 to 10 servings.

MIDDLE EASTERN LAMB SHISH KABOBS

Marinade

2 cups virgin olive oil
1 cup lemon juice
1/2 teaspoon sweet basil

2 cloves garlic, minced
1/2 teaspoon oregano
1/2 teaspoon black pepper

Kabobs

4 pounds lamb shoulder or leg, cut into 2-inch cubes
3 green peppers, seeded and cut into 2-inch chunks
3 large onions, cut into 2-inch chunks
8-ounces (or amount as needed) fresh white button mushrooms,
   cleaned and stems removed
3 large tomatoes, cut into quarters
Salt to taste
6 skewers (or more as needed)

Blend all the marinade ingredients in a large mixing bowl; add the cubed lamb and toss to completely cover. Tightly cover and marinate in the refrigerator overnight. Remove the lamb from the marinade, holding any remaining marinade aside. Preheat your broiler. Start to skewer the kabobs, alternating the meat with chunks of pepper, onion, tomato and mushrooms. Salt to taste. Brush the skewered meats and veggies with the reserved marinade, place on broiler rack about 4 inches from the heat. Broil 20 to 25 minutes for a medium-pink degree of doneness, a bit longer for well done. Brush with marinade throughout cooking and remember to turn skewers so that meat and vegetables cook evenly. Cooking over an open grill will take a little longer. Serve with white rice or couscous.
Yield: 6+ servings.

SAUTEED LAMB LIVER AND ONIONS

1/4 cup virgin olive oil (more as needed)
1 1/2 cups (more as needed) all-purpose flour
Salt to taste
Black pepper to taste
1 1/2 to 2 pounds lamb liver, sliced
1 onion, sliced thin
8 slices crisp bacon, crumbled (optional)

Most folk know only of calf liver prepared in this manner, but lamb liver is a wonderful alternative—very tender, not stringy or veiny, with a marvelous mild flavor. It is however, difficult to get because of minimal supply, unless ordered in advance. You won't find it in the meat case, but we think it's worth the "excursion into the unknown" to try it, so order it from your butcher. It's a favorite of mine.

Heat olive oil in a large skillet over medium low heat. Mix flour, salt and pepper; dredge the liver slices in the flour mixture and gently lay the slices into the skillet. Cook covered a few minutes until browned and sort of crispy on one side; turn slices over and top with onion slices, continuing to cook covered until browned and cooked through, about 3 to 5 minutes longer. If you prefer the onions a bit crispier, remove the liver, and continue cooking the onions to your preference. Remove to platter and top with the onions. If you prefer, you can top with crumbled pre-cooked bacon. Serve with a baked potato and fresh carrots.
Yield: 4 to 6 servings.

LEBANESE LAMB STEW

1/4 cup virgin olive oil
2 pounds lean shoulder lamb, cubed
2 onions, diced
2 cloves garlic, minced
3 cups water
1 teaspoon sweet basil
1 tablespoon fresh parsley, finely chopped
1 pound carrots, trimmed and cut into large pieces
1 bunch celery, trimmed and cut into large pieces (tops left whole)
2 turnips, trimmed and cut into large pieces
1 tablespoon all-purpose flour
1 cup water to blend flour
Salt to taste
Black pepper to taste

Heat oil over medium-high heat in a large stock or soup pot; sauté the lamb in the oil until browned on all sides and remove to a plate. Add the onions and garlic and sauté until golden, about 4 or 5 minutes. Add the 3 cups of water, basil, parsley, carrots, celery, turnips and lamb to the pot; cover and reduce to simmer very gently (adding more liquid as necessary) for 1 1/2 to 2 hours until lamb and veggies are tender. Blend the flour and remaining water and stir into the stew until thickened a bit; salt and pepper to taste. Remove from heat and serve over egg noodles and a tabbouleh salad.
Yield: 4 to 6 servings.

STUFFED BREAST OF LAMB

Stuffing

1 small onion, minced

2 stalks celery, minced

3/4 cup dry apricots, diced

1 cup regular white rice, uncooked

Black pepper to taste

1/2 cup fresh parsley, minced

2 cloves garlic, minced

1/4 cup virgin olive oil

1 snack-size box raisins

Salt to taste

2 cups water

2 tablespoons dry white wine

Glaze

1/2 cup butter, softened

1 tablespoon honey

2 cups apple cider + dashes of arrowroot or 2 tablespoons all-purpose flour

Dash nutmeg

2 pound breast of lamb

4 cups cooked apricots, pureed

Dash allspice

To prepare the lamb breast, have the butcher cut a pocket to free the meat from the ribs, for the full length of the roast, but not quite through the ends; also, to facilitate carving later, have him crack each rib joint, so slicing will go completely through.

Preheat the oven to 350 degrees. In a large skillet, sauté the garlic, onion and celery in oil over medium heat until lightly browned (5 to 10 minutes). Add the diced apricots, half the raisins, uncooked rice, salt and pepper, and sauté while stirring for about 3 minutes. Add the water, cover and lower heat to simmer for 10 minutes. Uncover and check to be sure all liquid is gone; if not, continue to stir and cook another couple of minutes. Mix in the parsley and wine and remove from the heat to thoroughly cool.

At this point, prepare a glaze (or buy one that's ready-made) by melting the butter in a saucepan over low heat; add in the glaze ingredients with the rest of the raisins, and blend while heating, using dashes of arrowroot or all-purpose flour to thicken just slightly if needed. Let cook for about 10 minutes, while stirring occasionally; remove from heat and keep warm. When stuffing mixture is thoroughly cooled, evenly fill the pocket in the lamb breast; use toothpicks to close the lamb tightly so stuffing does not escape. You can also lace the opening back and forth between the picks to ensure closure. Place the roast, pocket side up on a rack in a shallow roast pan; pour half the glaze over meat to coat. Bake for 2 hours or until desired doneness, remembering to baste frequently with the glaze. Remove from oven to a heated platter and let it set for a few minutes before slicing between each rib. Top individual servings with remainder of warm apricot sauce and serve with couscous or a rice pilaf.

Yield: 4 to 6 servings.

PORK

"Nothing in life is to be feared. It is only to be understood."
—Marie Curie

Often referred to as the "other white meat," pork is extremely nutritious and versatile, while being a good source of protein and fairly low in caloric content. Think of all the options: bacon, ham, ribs, roasts, sausage, chops and ground—all with tons of possible variations. We'll have difficulty covering them all, so remember your own creativity and put it to use, taking all the basics into consideration.

For seasonings, consider
...bay leaf, chives, cinnamon, cloves, garlic, ginger, lemon,
    orange, thyme, sage, rosemary and mace.

For great accompanying condiments, consider
...applesauce, cranberry sauce, mustards and various fruits.

Sauces might include
...sweet and sour, horseradish, barbeque or fruit sauces.

Gravies could include
...pan gravies or mushroom gravies.

Wonderful side dishes might include
... squash, potatoes, tomatoes or fruits.

When handling any fresh meat, as previously mentioned, remember to wash your hands before touching other items and thoroughly clean prep area to kill the bacteria that may be lurking.

Also, remember that pork should be cooked until well done, or at the very least medium-well done, so that no pink color remains. The interior temperature should register on the meat thermometer as approximately 180 degrees, except in precooked ham (140 degrees).

PORK ROAST CHART
(Times are approximate)

ROAST/WEIGHT	TIME PER LB./TEMP.	INTERNAL TEMP.
Center Pork Loin, 3- 5 pounds	30 min. @ 325°	170 to 180°
Half Pork Loin, 5-6 pounds	35 min. @ 325°	170 to 180°
Whole Ham (uncooked), 10-15 pounds	25 min. @ 325°	170 to 180°
Whole Ham (cooked), 10-15 pounds	15 min. @ 325°	130 to 140°
Half Ham (uncooked), 5-8 pounds	30 min. @ 325°	170 to 180°
Half Ham (cooked), 5-8 pounds	20 min. @ 325°	130 to 140°

ITALIAN-STYLE LOIN PORK CHOPS

1/4 cup virgin olive oil
8 thick-cut boneless loin pork chops
Non-stick cooking spray
3 cloves garlic, minced
1 onion, minced
8 cups marinara pasta sauce
8 ounces fresh white button mushrooms, sliced
Salt to taste
Black pepper to taste
Parmesan cheese to taste

Preheat the oven to 350 degrees. Heat oil in a large skillet over medium heat, browning chops 5 minutes per side; remove chops in a single layer to a large baking pan which has been sprayed with non-stick cooking spray. Using the same skillet, sauté the garlic and onion for a few minutes until golden. Add the pasta sauce, mushrooms, salt and pepper and heat through. Pour sauce and cheese to taste over chops and bake covered for an hour or until chops are tender. Serve with pasta tossed with garlic butter. Top with additional grated Parmesan cheese to taste.
Yield: 6 to 8 servings.

CUTLETS OF PORK WITH CRANBERRY

8 cutlets of pork loin
2 tablespoons virgin olive oil
2 cloves garlic, minced
Salt to taste
Black pepper to taste
1 cup dry white wine
1/2 cup water
1/4 cup orange honey
2 cups whole cranberry sauce
1/2 teaspoon ginger

In a large skillet over medium-low heat, sauté the cutlets in oil with the garlic, salt and pepper until nicely browned, about 7 or 8 minutes per side or until cooked through, adding a bit of the wine as needed to avoid burning. In a separate saucepan, combine the water, the rest of the wine, ginger, honey and the whole cranberry sauce, and heat thoroughly. Remove cutlets to a warm platter. Spoon sauce over pork as preferred and serve with a rice dish.
Yield: 4 servings.

BAKED STUFFED PORK CHOPS

Stuffing

    2 cloves garlic, minced

    1/2 cup celery, diced

    1 small onion, minced

    1 tablespoon virgin olive oil

    2 to 3 cups prepared boxed stuffing mix

    Salt to taste

    Black pepper to taste

    2 tablespoons orange zest or raisins

    1/4 cup water

Pork chops

    6 thick-cut, bone-in loin pork chops, slit to form a pocket

    1 tablespoon virgin olive oil

    Non-stick cooking spray

    1 14-ounce can chicken or vegetable consommé

    Salt to taste

    Black pepper to taste

Preheat the oven to 350 degrees. To prepare the stuffing, in a medium skillet sauté the garlic, celery and onion in the olive oil until onion is glassy, garlic browned, and celery fairly well cooked (about 10 minutes or less). In a mixing bowl, blend sautéed vegetables with stuffing mix; add salt, pepper, orange zest or raisins. Gently blend until well mixed, using just enough water to bind mix together. Spoon the mix into the pork chop pockets; secure the pockets closed with toothpicks and gently brown the chops over medium heat for about 5 to 8 minutes per side. Transfer chops to a baking dish, sprayed with cooking spray, placing chops "domino-style," with the top of one against bottom of the next. Add consommé, salt and pepper to taste. Cover and bake for 1 1/4 hours or until desired degree of doneness is reached, taking cover off the last 10 minutes. Nice served with creamed baby spinach and baked butternut squash.

Yield: 6 servings.

PORK LOIN CITRON

6 cups beef stock

1 cup onion, minced

1 tablespoon green chili pepper, chopped

1 tablespoon cornstarch

Salt to taste

2 pounds pork tenderloin

3 tablespoons virgin olive oil

1 orange, zest, juice and pulp

1 cup water

Black pepper to taste

Because the sauce takes a bit of preparation time, you should plan to begin making it ahead of time.

Boil the beef stock in a medium saucepan until it is reduced to about 2 1/2 cups, which should take about 45 minutes. Then, heat 1 tablespoon of the olive oil in a large skillet over medium-high heat. Sauté the onion until tender, and then add the reduced stock, the zest, juice and pulp of an orange, and the green peppers, and continue simmering until the mixture is reduced to 1 1/2 to 2 cups (which should take about 5 minutes longer). Blend the cornstarch and water together and whisk into the sauce mixture, stirring constantly until the sauce thickens a bit. Season as required with salt and pepper and set aside. Preheat your oven to 325 degrees. Sprinkle the pork tenderloin with salt and pepper, and brown on all sides in the remaining 3 tablespoons of oil in a skillet, for about 5 minutes. Insert a meat thermometer and transfer to a roast rack in a heavy ovenproof skillet and bake for approximately 1 hour, until the roast is cooked through or until the thermometer reads 170 degrees. Remove the roast and let it stand for 5 minutes before slicing. Meanwhile, bring the sauce back to a simmer to serve as an accent for the sliced roast.

Yield: 6 servings.

CRUSTED ROAST PORK LOIN DIJON

2 to 4 pounds pork tenderloin

4 cloves garlic, minced

2 tablespoons virgin olive oil

1 to 2 tablespoons fresh rosemary, chopped (or to taste)

Salt to taste

4 tablespoons Dijon mustard

Few small bay leaves, finely crumbled

2 tablespoons balsamic vinegar

Black pepper to taste

Preheat oven to 375 degrees. In a small bowl, blend mustard, garlic, bay leaves, olive oil, vinegar and rosemary; set aside. Dry the pork with paper toweling; sprinkle with salt and pepper and rub in. Then, spread the mustard mixture to completely cover the pork. Insert a meat thermometer into the roast and place pork roast in a baking dish on center oven rack, and roast until thermometer reads 170 degrees or to desired doneness (1 to 2 hours). Remove roast and let stand for approximately 15 minutes. Transfer to serving platter, slice and serve.

Yield: 4 to 8 servings.

MEDALLIONS OF PORK MILANAISE

1 cup Italian breadcrumbs

Black pepper to taste

1/2 teaspoon oregano

4 eggs, beaten

2 tablespoons virgin olive oil (more as needed)

2 cups marinara pasta sauce of your choice (more to taste)

Salt to taste

Garlic powder to taste

8 2-ounce pork loin slices

1 cup Parmesan cheese, grated

This dish only takes about 20 minutes to prepare and can be the star of a great quick meal.

In a large shallow dish, mix together breadcrumbs, salt, pepper, garlic powder and oregano. Dip the pork slices first in the egg, shaking off the excess; then, dredge the slices first in the cheese, then in the breadcrumb mix. Heat the olive oil in a large sauté pan over medium heat and cook slices a couple at a time until cooked through; keep warm in a low oven until ready to serve. Top with a little of the pasta sauce, heated. Great served with a salad and a fresh vegetable. Yield: 4 servings.

MEDALLIONS OF PORK à la MARCELLE

Medallions

2 1-pound pork tenderloins, each cut into 4 pieces

1/4 teaspoon ground cinnamon

1/4 cup fresh parsley, minced

Black pepper to taste

1 cup all-purpose flour

1 cup virgin olive oil

1/4 teaspoon nutmeg

Salt to taste

4 cups Italian seasoned breadcrumbs

2 large eggs, beaten

Sauce

1 to 2 cups sour cream

1/4 cup spicy French mustard

Place pork pieces flat between waxed paper sheets and pound to a thickness of about 1/2 inch using a meat mallet or a rolling pin. In a large shallow dish blend cinnamon, nutmeg, parsley, salt, pepper and breadcrumbs. Now, set up a "production line" in shallow dishes: the flour in one dish, the egg mixture in a second dish and the breadcrumb mixture in the third. Heat the oil in a large skillet or heavy fry pan over medium heat. Dredge (completely coat) each medallion in flour, shaking off the excess before coating with the egg mixture, followed by the breadcrumbs. Lay cutlets gently into the heated oil and cook each pork tenderloin piece about 2 minutes per side or until cooked through. Cook a couple of the pork tenderloin pieces at a time; as they're cooked, remove them to a platter and hold in a warm oven. Serve with fresh steamed asparagus and a starch of your choice. Before serving, blend the sour cream and mustard to serve as a sauce accent. Yield: 8 servings.

BAKED HAM À L'ABRICOT

Ham
  1/2 uncooked ham, butt end (5 to 7 pounds)
  Whole cloves, enough to stud top of ham

Glaze
  1 14-ounce can apricot halves, drained (or 2 oranges, sliced)
  1 cup apricot juice   1/2 cup packed brown sugar
  1 tablespoon orange honey   1/2 cup (1 stick) butter, softened
  Dash allspice   Dash ground cinnamon
  Dash ginger   Dash nutmeg
  1/4 cup raspberry vinaigrette dressing   1 tablespoon all-purpose flour
  1 cup water

Preheat the oven to 325 degrees. Remove any hard skin from the ham and use a knife to score a diamond pattern into the fat. Insert whole cloves into the diamonds and place the ham in a roasting pan, fat-side up, and roast for 30 minutes per pound or until the meat thermometer reads 160 degrees. Prepare the glaze so it's ready 30 minutes before the ham is to be done. In a medium saucepan, mix apricots or oranges, apricot juice, brown sugar, honey, butter, allspice, cinnamon, ginger, nutmeg and raspberry vinaigrette. In a small bowl blend flour and water and stir into the saucepan while simmering over very low heat. Cook 10 to 15 minutes or until glaze is slightly thickened. During the last half hour the ham is baking, baste frequently with the glaze. Let ham rest for 10 minutes before slicing and garnish with the apricot halves or orange slices and a bit of the remaining glaze. A nice variation on an old tradition; great with baked yams.
Yield: 12+ servings.

FRUITED PORK TENDERLOIN

  2 pork tenderloins (about 3 pounds total)   Salt to taste
  Black pepper to taste   2 cloves garlic, slivered
  Bacon strips, raw (to be used if pork is very lean;   1 snack-sized box raisins
  enough to cover tops of tenderloins lengthwise)
  1 24-ounce jar cinnamon applesauce
  1 apple, cored and cut into thin wedges

Preheat the oven to 325 degrees. Use salt and pepper to season pork tenderloins; cut small slits in the top of each loin and insert the garlic slivers. Place the loins on a rack in a shallow roast pan, (top with bacon if pork is very lean, to keep from drying out; if bacon is used, remove during the last 15 minutes of cooking). Bake 1 1/2 hours or until a meat thermometer inserted in the thickest part of the loin registers 170 degrees, or cooked to your preference. Remove the roasts to a warm platter and let them set up for 10 or 15 minutes. In a small saucepan, heat the applesauce and raisins until very hot. Slice the roast and plate individually, alternating slices of roast with wedges of apple. Top with applesauce according to your preference and serve. Nice with garlic mashed potatoes.
Yield: 6 servings.

HAM CALZONES

    2 tablespoons virgin olive oil
    1 cup lean cooked ham, diced
    1 green bell pepper, diced
    1 small onion, minced
    2 cloves garlic, minced
    Salt to taste
    Black pepper to taste
    1/2 cup ricotta cheese
    1/2 cup mozzarella cheese, shredded
    1 tube refrigerator pizza dough
    Flour as needed to prepare surface
    Water as needed to crimp calzone edges
    Cornmeal as needed to prepare baking sheet
    2 tablespoons butter, melted

Preheat oven to 500 degrees. Heat oil in a large skillet over medium heat; add the ham, peppers, onions, garlic, salt and pepper. Sauté 2 to 4 minutes, until ham is heated through and onion and garlic are golden; remove from the heat and add the cheeses, blending everything together. Lightly flour a flat preparation surface; lay out the pizza dough on it, dividing it into 4 sections. Using a rolling pin, roll or flatten each section into a 6-inch circle. Divide the filling into the center of each piece of dough and then fold the dough over to form a crescent shape. Crimp the edges closed, using a bit of water to seal the edges. Sprinkle cornmeal on a baking sheet, place calzones on the sheet and bake for about 10 minutes, brushing tops with melted butter as they bake, until golden brown. Makes a nice luncheon with a salad.
Yield: 4 servings.

PORK CHOPS WITH SAUERKRAUT

    6 large rib or loin pork chops
    Non-stick cooking spray
    Salt to taste
    Black pepper to taste
    2 cloves garlic, minced
    1 pound prepared sauerkraut, undrained

Preheat oven to 350 degrees. Place chops in a single layer in a shallow baking dish sprayed with non-stick cooking spray. Dust chops with salt and pepper; sprinkle a bit of garlic on each chop. Bake uncovered for 30 minutes and remove from the pan, draining excess fat drippings. Layer the undrained sauerkraut in the bottom of the pan and top with the chops, turned to the second side. Season with a bit more salt and pepper if desired, and bake uncovered an additional 30 minutes, or until chops are very tender.
Yield: 6 servings.

PORK CHOP SUEY

3 tablespoons virgin olive oil
1 large onion, minced
1 clove garlic, minced
3 cups vegetable or chicken broth
1 teaspoon sugar
4 tablespoons soy sauce
1 8-ounce can water chestnuts, sliced
2 to 3 cups leftover pork (or chicken or beef), diced
1 cup cooked and drained carrots, chopped
1 cup cooked and drained celery, chopped
1 cup canned peas, drained
3 tablespoons cornstarch
2 cups cold water
1 pound fresh bean sprouts, rinsed and drained

If you have a wok handy, this is the time to use it (if not, a large skillet will do).

Heat olive oil over moderate flame; add the onion and garlic and stir fry for a few minutes. Add the broth, sugar, soy sauce, water chestnuts, meat, carrots, celery and peas and return to simmer. Blend the cornstarch and water in a small bowl and add to the meat mixture, stirring gently until thickened. Add the bean sprouts and stir to heat through. Serve with fried rice.
Yield: 4 to 6 servings.

PORK FRIED RICE

3 tablespoons virgin olive oil
1 medium onion, minced
1 clove garlic, minced
8 ounces fresh white button mushrooms, cleaned and sliced
3 tablespoons soy sauce
Dash black pepper
3 cups cooked rice, heated
1 cup diced cooked pork, heated
3 eggs, scrambled and kept warm

Heat olive oil in a wok or large skillet sauté onion, garlic, mushrooms, soy sauce and pepper over moderate heat for 5 minutes or until lightly browned. When thoroughly heated, add the mixture to the heated and precooked rice, pork and egg; mix well. This is nice with chop suey.
Yield: 4 to 6 servings.

HAM CASSEROLE

4 cups cooked ham, cubed
8 ounces fresh white button mushrooms, cleaned and sliced
2 cups cooked peas or green beans
Non-stick cooking spray
4 medium potatoes, scrubbed or peeled and sliced
4 tablespoons butter
3 tablespoons pre-sifted flour
Salt to taste
Black pepper to taste
4 cups heavy cream
Seasoned breadcrumbs to taste

Admittedly this is a bit high in calories, but it's a great way to use up leftover ham.

Preheat oven to 375 degrees. In a large bowl, mix ham, mushrooms and peas or beans. Spray a large casserole dish with cooking spray; put one layer of one-third of the sliced potatoes in the bottom of the dish, followed by a layer of half the ham-vegetable mixture. In a separate pan, heat the butter over moderately low heat, and whisk in the flour, salt and pepper, and blend until smooth; slowly add cream, whisking continuously until the mixture is smooth and has thickened a bit. Pour some of the mix over the first layers. Add another layer of potatoes and the rest of the ham-vegetable mix, and a bit more of the sauce. Put a final layer of potatoes in the dish and topped with the rest of the sauce, making sure sauce completely covers the layers; top with breadcrumbs. Cover and cook for about an hour until potatoes are fork tender. Serve with a nice green salad.
Yield: 4 to 6 servings.

✓ HELPFUL HINTS - (Stuff your grandma should have told you!)

- Use a meat baster to "squeeze" pancake batter onto the griddle; perfectly shaped pancakes every time.
- To remove burned food from your skillet, simply add a few drops of dishwashing liquid to the pan and enough water just to cover the bottom of the pan; bring it to a boil (watch it, this will heat up fast). The offending chunks should float away.
- If you wrap celery in aluminum foil when you refrigerate it, it will last for weeks.
- You say your gravy is lumpy? Pour it through a sieve, mashing the lumps out. Return gravy to pan and slowly reheat.
- Frequently, there will be too much fat in the gravy; to solve the problem, remember that fat rises to the surface, so cool the gravy, remove the excess fat and reheat the gravy before serving.

POULTRY: henhouse hotties

"Only those who risk find out how far one can go."
—T. S. Eliot

It's time now for nature's own "cluck for a buck," so let's go to the barnyard.

So, just why did the chicken cross the road? Perhaps she was being chased by one of our ancient ancestors, whose intentions were to get her into a pot and then onto some sort of table.

Actually, the Chinese probably can claim its origin, gradually sending it on, as they did so many things, through Asia to Greco-Roman tables. For American tables, variations on chicken have claimed the No. 1 spot on the list of "most popular" poultry…with turkey a close second, and duck, Rock Cornish game hen and squab hens following closely behind.

In the interest of not inundating you with facts, procedures and terminology, we have chosen to supply you with the simple basics. Poultry today comes to us usually ready to prepare and available whole, cut into parts, and packaged in segments such as breasts, legs, etc., so taking the time to learn how to clean, dress and cut up poultry seems unnecessary.

However, one extremely important thing to remember is: When handling uncooked poultry (as with ANY raw meat, eggs or seafood) - WASH YOUR HANDS FREQUENTLY, especially before touching any OTHER items. Clean preparation surfaces thoroughly before using that surface to prepare other foods. Improper cleaning can transfer the bacteria from one place to another and hangs out the "Welcome" sign, inviting bacteria to enter your body for a field day.

For this volume, we'll concentrate on preparation of chicken and turkey, leaving the less-frequent preparation of duck, goose and squab for another time.

For CHICKEN, there are a variety of methods of preparation, such as:

ROASTING: Since most whole chickens come to the local market already cleaned, dressed and ready to go, they need only to be rinsed, dried and stuffed (if you wish) using about 1/2 cup of stuffing per pound of chicken. Prepare stuffing according to package directions (maybe think about adding chopped celery and onion to the mix), and then—just before the chicken goes into the oven—stuff the bird loosely into both the neck and body cavities. (See Roast Chicken, page 115). Under NO circumstances, should you let uncooked, stuffed chicken set at room temperature for ANY length of time (remember the bacteria). Your oven should be preheated from 325 degrees for a larger bird (5 pounds or more) to 400 degrees for a smaller chicken. Roast for approximately 1 to 1/2 hours for smaller chickens to 1 1/2 to 3 hours or more for larger ones. The key? Make sure the meat is cooked to an internal temperature of 190 degrees. It's always wise to use a meat thermometer when roasting poultry; insert the thermometer into the thigh or deep into the center of the stuffing for correct results.

FRYING: To many of us, deep-fried chicken represents all that is "finger-licking" good in the world, and while calorically or "cholesterol-ically" we should perhaps reconsider this particular type of preparation, we'll list it as one of life's little pleasures.

SAUTEING: Coat the chicken pieces according to recipe, while heating a sufficient amount—about 3/4 to 1 inch—of olive oil or cooking oil in a large skillet. Add the chicken and cook uncovered about 20 minutes on each side, being careful not to let the pieces burn by adjusting the heat as necessary. Drain the chicken pieces on paper towels. While in reality this is another method of FRYING, sautéing may be interpreted in other ways according to other recipe requirements, as you will note.

STEWING: This is an ideal way to use up leftover chicken or turkey. To make an excellent soup, start by putting the leftover carcass (sans stuffing) into a large soup pot. Add a bit of salt and pepper and a small chopped onion, and cover with cold water; bring to a boil—then lower to simmer until all the meat has left the bones. Remove the pieces of carcass, saving all the meat to one side. Strain the remaining liquid into another pot; add the vegetables of your choice: carrots, potatoes, onion, celery, green beans, zucchini, etc., with a large can of crushed tomatoes and the chicken. Adjust seasonings to your taste and simmer until cooked to perfection. Stews are best cooked ahead of time, and served reheated the next day.

For TURKEY, the primary method of preparation is:

ROASTING: A medium-sized, ready-to-cook turkey is usually 10 to 20 pounds. A young hen or tom that is very tender is considered the very best for roasting. Directions are much the same as for a roasted chicken. Many turkeys today are brought to market frozen, and must be defrosted properly prior to roasting. If, for instance, you wish to prepare the frozen bird later in the afternoon, let the wrapped bird sit in the sink covered with cold water. Change the water frequently. Defrosting the bird by this method will take several hours, so start early. You might also wish to defrost the turkey in the refrigerator, following directions on the packaging. While this takes longer, it is the safest method. Once defrosted, make sure that the cavities are emptied of giblets, etc., and set aside for use in preparing the gravy or for soup stock. Leftover turkey can be used in numerous ways such as soups, sandwiches, fried cutlets, croquettes, à la king, hash or salads. Truly a versatile meat.

ROAST TURKEY

Turkey and stuffing

1 20-pound tom turkey
4 6-ounce bags seasoned stuffing mix
2 cups onion, diced

Salt to taste
2 cups celery, diced
1/4 pound butter, melted for basting

Gravy

Reserved giblets, heart, neck and liver of turkey, rinsed
1 quart water
1 onion, cut in chunks
3 carrots, cleaned, trimmed and cut in chunks
2 stalks celery, cleaned, trimmed and cut in chunks
2 whole bay leaves
Salt to taste
Black pepper to taste
Minced garlic to taste
6 tablespoons all-purpose flour (vary amount as needed)
1 cup dry white wine

Preheat oven to 325 degrees. Defrost bird as suggested. Remove cavity contents and rinse the bird inside and out with cold water, pat dry inside and out and salt cavity. Prepare stuffing per package directions, adding 2 cups each of diced onion and celery. Loosely stuff both cavities so that stuffing can expand during cooking. Secure the body and neck cavities closed with a very simple truss needle kit available at any market. Tuck the wing tips against the body of the bird and tent the tips loosely with foil to prevent burning during the first few hours of cooking. Tie the legs together with white twine. Place the bird on a rack in a shallow roast pan, breast side up, and with a meat thermometer in its thigh or deep into the stuffing, being sure it does not touch any bone. Popup indicators, which are placed into the breast, are also now readily available to indicate when the bird is done. Roast uncovered, but if the turkey starts to brown too quickly, form a tent over the top loosely with foil, removing it toward the end of cooking. Turkey should be basted frequently with butter or margarine and natural juices, using a basting tube. A 20-pound bird should cook in 6 1/2 to 7 hours, to an internal temperature of 180 degrees (that's about 15 to 20 minutes per pound). When the bird is finished, set on a platter and cover with foil, to allow it to rest for 15 to 20 minutes before slicing.

For a nice GRAVY, start this process about 4 1/2 hours into the roasting time. Wash the giblets, heart, livers and neck, and simmer in 1 quart of cold water for about 15 to 25 minutes with a large, coarsely chopped onion, carrots, celery, bay leaves, salt, pepper and garlic to taste. Then remove the neck and heart, and continue to gently simmer the remaining giblets and livers for about 1 1/2 to 2 hours, being sure to replenish the liquid as necessary. Take off fire and remove the bay leaf, carrots, onions and celery, and discard. Remove and dice the giblets and livers and set aside; reserve the stock liquid. Skim fat from the pan juices and reserve about a half cup. Next, add wine into the roast pan and deglaze it (over low heat, scrape up the bits and stir with the wine); remove from the heat and hold aside. In a separate saucepan, return the reserved fat and just enough flour to thicken, whisking constantly for about 3 or 4 minutes until smooth (careful now, you're not making glue). Whisk in the reserved wine and about 4 to 5 cups of the stock and simmer for about 5 more minutes, whisking occasionally. Adjust seasonings to taste, and add the reserved giblets and livers, and keep warm until served.

Yield of turkey: 15 to 20 servings + leftovers.

Yield of gravy: 6 to 7 cups.

FRIED CHICKEN

Sufficient cooking oil to cover chicken
1 small to medium chicken, cut into parts
1 egg, beaten
1/2 cup milk
1 1/2 cups all-purpose flour
1 1/2 teaspoons salt
1/2 teaspoon black pepper, coarsely ground
Dash of garlic powder
Other seasonings of choice

Heat oil in a deep fryer and, using a thermometer, bring oil to a temperature of 350 degrees. Start with a small to medium chicken, cut into parts. In a small bowl, blend the egg and milk. In a clean paper bag, mix flour, salt, pepper, garlic powder and other seasonings of your choice. When oil reaches required temperature, dip the individual chicken pieces, a few at a time, into the egg mixture and shake off the excess; then drop individual pieces into the flour mixture and coat thoroughly. Fry just a few pieces at a time for 15 to 20 minutes until golden brown or cooked through. Remove chicken to drain on paper toweling and move to a low oven to keep warm.
Don't forget to lick your fingers!
Yield: 4 to 6 servings.

SAUTEED CHICKEN LIVERS

Virgin olive oil as needed for frying
1 medium onion, chopped
1 clove garlic, minced
8 ounces fresh white button mushrooms, cleaned and sliced
Salt to taste
Black pepper to taste
1 to 1 1/2 pounds chicken livers, rinsed and drained
Heavy splash red or white wine

Add enough olive oil to cover the bottom of a heavy skillet. Over moderate heat, delicately sauté the onions, garlic and mushrooms, lightly seasoning with salt and pepper about 5 to 7 minutes covered. Add the chicken livers and cook covered about 5 minutes longer until they are cooked through. Add the wine to the skillet and continue to cook over high heat a few minutes more until most of the liquid is gone. Serve over rice.
Yield: 6 to 8 servings.

HONEY ORANGE MUSTARD CHICKEN

2 pounds skinless chicken breasts (about 4 half breasts)
1/2 cup honey
1/4 cup Dijon mustard
1/2 tablespoon sweet basil
Dash salt
Black pepper to taste
1 clove garlic, minced
1 cup orange juice
1 tablespoon grated orange zest (grated orange peel)

Preheat oven to 400 degrees. In a medium bowl, prepare sauce by blending honey, mustard, basil, salt, pepper, garlic, orange juice and zest. Brush chicken breasts with the sauce on both sides and place in a large, shallow baking dish. Top all chicken pieces with the remaining sauce, and bake uncovered for 20 to 30 minutes or until thoroughly cooked. *No "cluck for a buck" here!*
Yield: 4 servings.

CHICKEN BREAST PICCATA CUTLETS

1 1/2 to 2 pounds boneless, skinless chicken breast halves (about 4)

3 tablespoons butter	3 tablespoons virgin olive oil
1 egg, beaten	1/4 cup flour
Salt to taste	Black pepper to taste
3/4 cup dry white wine	Fresh chopped parsley to taste
5 tablespoons lemon juice	Lemon slices to cover

Cooked slices of turkey breast may be substituted for chicken in this recipe. If using cooked turkey, don't pound the meat.

Place chicken breasts on a cutting board; cover with plastic wrap and pound with a mallet to make a cutlet approximately 1/4 - to - 1/2 inch thick. Melt butter into the oil and heat in a large skillet over medium-high heat. Beat egg in a small shallow bowl. In another shallow bowl, blend flour, salt and pepper. Dip chicken into the egg and lightly coat with the flour mixture. Carefully add poultry slices to the skillet and cook for 2 to 4 minutes per side, or until surface is browned and the meat cooked through. Immediately remove the poultry cutlets to drain on paper toweling and then to a platter to keep warm. Rid the skillet of most of the fat; add the wine and parsley to the pan and scrape up meat bits while cooking over lower heat. Remove from the heat and add the lemon juice. Return to heat and cook sauce for a few minutes, until slightly reduced. Drizzle sauce over the top of the cutlets on a platter. Top with slices of lemon and serve.
Yield: 4 servings.

CHICKEN BREAST GRILL

1 cup red wine 1 teaspoon horseradish
2 cloves garlic, minced (more to your taste)
1 cup tomato catsup Salt to taste
Black pepper to taste
1 1/2 to 2 pounds boneless, skinless, chicken breast halves (about 4)

Make marinade by combining wine, horseradish, garlic, catsup, salt and pepper. Use enough of the marinade to coat chicken breasts well; reserve remaining marinade to use during grilling. Cover and refrigerate chicken breasts and marinate for 5 to 10 minutes. If using an outside grill, fire it up—or, if broiling, heat the broiler. Place chicken breasts on the grill about 6 inches from a moderate heat source and cook 30 to 60 minutes or until juices run clear. If using the broiler, cook about 15 to 20 minutes until cooked through. Be sure to baste them often with the reserved portion of the marinade, heating what is left to top off the finished chicken breasts. A bit spicy for some, but a great dish served with rice or pasta al olio.
Yield: 4 servings.

ROAST CHICKEN

Chicken
1 3 1/2 to 4-pound roasting chicken 1/2 teaspoon salt
1/2 teaspoon thyme 1 onion, cubed large
1 to 2 stalks celery, trimmed and sliced into large chunks
1 tablespoon butter (or substitute prepared boxed stuffing mix if preferred)
Water for roast pan
Gravy
1 tablespoon flour (per cup of pan juice and water)
Water to blend flour

Rinse cavity and outside of chicken in cold water and pat dry, while preheating oven to 475 degrees. Rub inside cavity of chicken with salt and thyme; add onion and celery and butter (or prepared stuffing mix, if preferred). Rub a bit more butter over exterior of chicken; place chicken on a roast rack in the roasting pan, breast-side down with wings tucked to the back. Add just enough water to cover the bottom of the pan, and roast for about 10 to 15 minutes. Reduce the oven temperature to 325 degrees and continue to roast for another 15 to 20 minutes. Turn the chicken over to breast side up, and roast until it is brown, another 60 to 70 minutes or until meat thermometer reads 190 degrees. Cooked this way, the chicken should be nice and crisp on the outside, while retaining its juices. Remove chicken and cover with foil to set about 5 minutes.

If gravy is desired, stir the flour into pan juices (1 tablespoon per cup of pan juices and water); blend using a whisk directly in the roasting pan over medium heat. Whisk continuously to avoid lumping. Cook until thickened to desired consistency. A great dish served with oven-browned or baked potatoes and a fresh vegetable.
Yield: 4 to 5 servings with leftovers.

CHICKEN FINGERS MOUTARD

1 1/2 to 2 pounds boneless, skinless chicken breast halves
(or use the frozen variety, already cut into strips)

1 cup all-purpose flour	1/2 teaspoon salt
1/2 teaspoon black pepper	Garlic powder to taste
3/4 cup milk	1 cup virgin olive oil
1/3 cup orange honey	1/2 cup spicy brown mustard

Use prepared chicken strips, or cut chicken breasts into 1/2 inch strips. Blend flour, salt and pepper (and garlic powder if you like) in a large plastic storage bag. Dip the chicken strips in milk, and then place them in the bag with the flour mix to coat them well. Remove and hold on waxed paper or a plate. Heat oil in large skillet or fry pan to 350 degrees (a good test is to place a small bit of white bread into the heated oil; if it browns nicely in a minute or so it's ready). Gently place chicken pieces into heated oil for about 3 minutes each side or until crisply done, making sure not to crowd them. While cooking, blend mustard and honey for dipping sauce, and serve with the crisp chicken fingers after they have been drained on paper toweling.

Yield: 4 entrée servings; 6 to 10 appetizer servings.

POULET À L'ORANGE

2 1/2 to 3 pounds boneless, skinless chicken breast halves (6 half breasts)
4 tablespoons virgin olive oil (more as needed)
Salt to taste
Black pepper to taste
2 cloves garlic, minced (more to taste)
1 onion, minced
1/2 cup dry white wine
1/2 cup orange juice
12 slices fresh orange

Add chicken to a large skillet, sautéing in oil until lightly browned on both sides. Sprinkle with salt and pepper; top with onion, garlic and wine, and continue to sauté covered for another 5 minutes. Add orange juice and orange slices and cook covered over medium heat for another 15 minutes or until thoroughly cooked. Remove chicken to platter and top with the pan juices and orange slices. Serve with pilaf and a fresh vegetable.

Yield: 6 servings.

CHICKEN BREASTS CITRON

Marinade

1/4 cup lemon juice

2 tablespoons garlic, minced

1 small bunch fresh parsley, minced

Salt to taste

Grated zest (rind) of 1 lemon

1/2 cup orange juice

Black pepper to taste

Chicken

1 1/2 to 2 pounds boneless, skinless chicken breast halves, rinsed and patted dry (4 half breasts)

4 tablespoons virgin olive oil (more as needed)

1/2 to 1 cup all-purpose flour

1 cup chicken broth

Mix all the marinade ingredients and blend well. Coat the chicken breasts thoroughly with the marinade in a shallow dish, cover and refrigerate for 2 hours. When ready to proceed, preheat the oven to 350 degrees. Remove the chicken from the marinade, draining any excess (reserve marinade for later use). Heat the oil in a large fry pan over medium heat; dredge the chicken in flour and brown on all sides for a few minutes. Transfer chicken to a shallow baking dish (about 9-by-13 inches); top with chicken broth and the marinade and bake for about 1 hour or until tender, basting occasionally with the pan juices. Great with garlic mashed potatoes and fresh carrots Vichy. Yield: 4 servings.

CHICKEN BREAST VERONIQUE

4 tablespoons virgin olive oil (more as needed)

2 tablespoons butter

1 clove garlic, minced

1/4 cup scallions (or onions), finely chopped

1 1/2 to 2 pounds boneless, skinless chicken breast halves, rinsed and patted dry (4 half breasts)

Salt to taste

Black pepper to taste

1/2 cup chicken broth

1/2 cup white wine

1/2 cup heavy cream

2 cups seedless green grapes

Heat the oil and butter in a large skillet over medium heat until butter is melted. Sauté the garlic and scallions a few minutes, until garlic is golden. Add the chicken, seasoned with salt and pepper, to the skillet; sauté until chicken is browned on both sides (about 5 minutes), adding a bit more oil to prevent burning if needed. Remove chicken to a warm platter. Lower heat to simmer and gradually whisk in the broth, wine and cream; bring to a boil and again reduce to simmer. Add the chicken and spoon-baste the sauce to cover. Simmer covered until cooked through (about another 10 to 15 minutes). Add the grapes during the last 5 minutes of cooking. Yield: 4 servings.

POULET À L'ABRICOT

1 1/2 to 2 pounds boneless, skinless chicken breast halves (4 half breasts)

1/2 cup soy sauce   Zest of 1 lemon

4 tablespoons virgin olive oil (more as needed)

1 clove garlic, minced   1/4 cup celery, diced

1/2 cup onion diced   1/4 cup chicken or vegetable broth

1/2 cup apricot juice   1 tablespoon lemon juice

1/2 teaspoon salt   1/4 teaspoon black pepper

10 to 12 cooked apricot halves

For those who don't like apricots, you may substitute other fruits and juices (pears, plum, pineapple, etc.) Be creative!

Cover chicken with soy sauce mixed with half of the zest, and let it sit covered and refrigerated 20 to 30 minutes. Heat oil in a large fry pan or skillet over medium heat, adding the garlic, celery and onion to sauté until celery is tender and onion is glassy. Add the chicken to the skillet and sauté for 4 or 5 minutes, adding a bit of the broth if needed to prevent burning. Then add remaining broth, apricot juice, lemon juice and remaining zest. Season with salt and pepper to taste, cover and simmer over medium low-heat another 10 to 15 minutes, topping with the apricot halves during the last five minutes of cooking. Check for sufficient liquid and add more juice as needed. When done, remove chicken to a warm platter, and top with remaining sauce.
Yield: 4 servings.

CHICKEN BREASTS ITALIA

2 tablespoons virgin olive oil (more as needed)

2 pounds boneless, skinless chicken breasts, cubed (4 to 5 half breasts)

2 cloves garlic, minced   4 to 6 raw Idaho potatoes, peeled and cubed

1 medium onion, diced   1 green bell pepper, cored and diced

1 29-ounce can of crushed Italian style tomatoes, or if you prefer, your favorite prepared chunky pasta sauce

1/2 teaspoon sweet basil   Salt to taste

Black pepper to taste   Water to steam

1 pound green asparagus spears

Heat olive oil in a large skillet or sauté pan; sauté the chicken and garlic over medium heat until lightly browned. Add the potatoes, onion and peppers and continue cooking covered for an additional 5 minutes, stirring occasionally. Add the tomatoes, basil, salt and pepper and bring to a boil; reduce heat to medium; cover and simmer gently for 30 minutes, or until potatoes and chicken are tender, gently stirring occasionally. In another pan, steam the asparagus spears for about 15 minutes until crisply tender and remove from heat. Serve chicken with a rice dish and the steamed asparagus spears topped with melted butter. *A total meal.*
Yield: 4 to 6 servings.

CHICKEN BREASTS ITALIAN (variation)

Non-stick cooking spray
2 1/2 to 3 pounds boneless, skinless chicken breast halves (6 half breasts)
1 tablespoon Italian seasoning spice blend
2 cups Italian-style breadcrumbs
4 eggs, beaten
1 cup Provolone cheese, shredded
1/2 cup Feta cheese, crumbled

Preheat the oven to 325 degrees and spray a 2-by-9-by-13-inch baking pan with cooking spray. Rinse the chicken breasts in cold water and pat dry. Mix the seasonings and breadcrumbs (this is easy to do using a large, clean plastic storage bag); dip the chicken breasts in beaten eggs, shaking off excess; then shake in bag of crumbs. Place in baking pan and generously top with a combination of the cheeses. Cover and bake for a half hour; uncover and bake an additional 15 minutes or until chicken is cooked through. This goes great with pasta and a basil marinara sauce.
Yield: 6 servings.

CHICKEN MUSHROOM DIVINE

1 cup water
1 tablespoon all-purpose flour
1 14-ounce can cream of mushroom soup
1 cup heavy cream
1/4 cup mayonnaise
Heavy splash dry sherry
Dash nutmeg
1/2 teaspoon salt
1 teaspoon black pepper
Non-stick cooking spray
1 10-ounce package frozen broccoli florets or spears, thawed
2 1/2 to 3 pounds boneless, skinless chicken breast halves (6 half breasts)
Virgin olive oil to sauté chicken
8 ounces fresh white button mushrooms, cleaned and sliced
1/4 cup Parmesan or Asiago cheese, grated

Preheat oven to 350 degrees. Combine and blend flour and water; then blend with soup, cream, mayonnaise, sherry, nutmeg and salt and pepper in a large mixing bowl. Spray a 2-by-9-by-13-inch casserole dish with cooking spray; spread the broccoli on the bottom. In a separate skillet, briefly sauté chicken on all sides in oil; then place the chicken breasts on top of the broccoli and the mushrooms on top of the chicken. Pour the soup mixture over the chicken to cover and sprinkle with cheese. Bake 45 minutes or until chicken is tender. Wonderful with a rice dish.
Yield: 6 servings.

CHICKEN MARENGO

3 tablespoons virgin olive oil (more as needed)	
1 3-pound broiler, cut into quarters	2 small onions, diced
1 tablespoon all-purpose flour	1 cup water
1/2 cup chicken consommé	1 14-ounce can pureed tomatoes
2 cloves garlic, minced	1/4 teaspoon thyme
1 whole bay leaf	Salt to taste
Black pepper to taste	1/2 cup dry white wine
8 ounces white button mushrooms, sliced	1 tablespoon fresh parsley, chopped

Heat the olive oil in a large skillet, and cook the chicken pieces until browned on all sides; then remove the chicken to a warm platter. Reduce heat to simmer; add the onion to skillet and cook until just slightly browned. Whisk in the blended flour and water and stir continuously while cooking an additional 3 or 4 minutes. Add the consommé, tomatoes, garlic, thyme, bay leaf, salt, pepper and wine, and bring to a boil. Reduce again to simmer; add the reserved chicken and cover, cooking until meat is tender (about a half hour). Remove the chicken pieces to a platter, keeping warm. Add the mushrooms to the sauce, and continue simmering for another 5 minutes. When finished, pour sauce over chicken to completely cover; top with parsley and serve. *This dish is named for the hastily prepared meal that Napoleon ate after his 1800 victory at the battle of Marengo in northern Italy.*
Yield: 4 servings.

ORANGE CRANBERRY CHICKEN

1 1/2 to 2 pounds boneless, skinless chicken breasts halves (4 half breasts)
Non-stick cooking spray
1 small onion, minced
1 tablespoon fresh parsley, minced
2 cups whole cranberry sauce
1 1/2 cups orange juice
Salt to taste
Black pepper to taste
4 fresh orange slices

Place the chicken in a covered casserole sprayed with cooking spray. Combine the onion, parsley, cranberry sauce, orange juice, salt and pepper; pour mixture over chicken breasts and top breasts with orange slices. Completely and tightly cover the casserole, and set it in the refrigerator for 5 to 6 hours. Just prior to cooking, preheat your oven to 325 or 350 degrees. When ready to cook, cover loosely with foil and place in oven; cook for 1 1/4 to 1 1/2 hours, or until the chicken is cooked and tender. Goes nicely with baked potatoes and squash.
Yield: 4 servings.

COQ AU VIN

6 tablespoons virgin olive oil (more as needed)
1 3-pound broiler, quartered (or substitute 4 boneless, skinless chicken breasts)
1/2 cup onion, finely diced
1 tablespoon all-purpose flour
3/4 cup chicken consommé
3/4 cup red wine (more as needed)
2 cloves garlic, minced
1 whole bay leaf
Heavy dash of thyme
1 16-ounce jar baby onions, drained
2 cups fresh white button mushrooms, sliced
Salt to taste
Black pepper to taste

Here's another traditional French favorite. While coq in French is "rooster," Coq au Vin translates to "chicken in wine sauce."

Heat the olive oil in a heavy skillet over medium heat, add the chicken pieces and brown on all sides. Remove and hold chicken aside. Add chopped onion to skillet and cook until just glassy. Now, whisk in and blend the flour and brown; add the consommé, wine, garlic, bay leaf, thyme, baby onions and mushrooms. Return the chicken to the skillet, cover and bring to a boil; reduce to simmer covered for 45 minutes to an hour or until meat is tender. Add more wine as needed during cooking. Season with salt and pepper to taste. Wonderful served with boiled parsley potatoes and a glass of a full-bodied red wine, such as a burgundy or a cabernet. (Don't forget to remove the bay leaf prior to serving – not too great for the dental work!)
Yield: 4 servings.

☑ ■■■■■■■■■■■■■■■■■■■■
HELPFUL HINTS - (Stuff your grandma should have told you!)

■ You've brewed some delicious coffee to accompany dessert, but it seems the coffee is weak – don't throw it out. Add a bit of instant coffee to the pot. The quality of taste will be virtually the same, but a lot stronger.

■ Try microwaving your fresh or frozen vegetables in a covered glass or ceramic bowl. Do NOT add any water or other liquid – they will cook in their own juices. Season to taste and serve.

■ For mashed potatoes, try cooking them in chicken broth instead of water. Save a bit of the broth to use in place of milk or cream when whipping.

■ ■ ■ ■ ■ ■ ■ ■ ■ ■ ■ ■ ■ ■ ■ ■ ■ ■

FISH & SHELLFISH: hook, line & sinker

"Faith in oneself is the best and safest course."
—Michelangelo

When discussing fresh and salt water fish and seafood, it basically falls into one of two categories: fish or shellfish.

Shellfish, of course, include crabs, shrimp, lobster and clams, as well as oysters and scallops (the latter actually are classified as mollusks). With shellfish, freshness is optimum (use live lobsters, for instance, if available).

Fish have fins and gills (such as tuna, mackerel, flounder, salmon, haddock, cod, sole, snapper, swordfish, bass and trout) and inhabit both fresh and salt waters. Whether choosing a delicate fish (such as sole) or a stronger-flavored fish (such as shark), you MUST be sure that the fish is absolutely fresh (or fresh and "flash frozen"), has no foul odor and is firm. Frozen fish should be defrosted just prior to use and NEVER refrozen.

What is the best preparation method for fish and shellfish? There are many answers to that question.

To be sure fish is properly cooked, the magic test is to observe when the flesh becomes flaky and changes from translucent to opaque. At that point, it is done and should not be cooked more.

Fish may be baked, fried, sautéed, broiled, grilled, steamed or poached. With shellfish and mollusks, your choices also are multiple: baking, boiling, steaming, frying, sautéing and more. In the following recipes, we will try to cover a few of the many preparation methods.

Freshwater fish and seafood are wonderful low-cal sources of protein and minerals and a delicate change of pace from red meats and poultry. Just conjure up a Maine lobster, Alaskan king crab, baked salmon and (for those who are a bit more daring) sushi.

When preparing fish and seafood, consider using some of these popular spices and herbs, with delicate fish and shellfish: thyme, ginger, dill, tarragon, fennel, chives and bay leaves. For heartier fish, consider using curry, rosemary, sage or oregano. Garnishes such as lemon, cherry tomatoes, cucumber slices, radishes and parsley are very popular.

Because fish and seafood today are brought to market cleaned, filleted and fresh, we won't go into the details of cleaning and preparing fish and shellfish. Just be sure to tell your market salesperson what you intend to prepare, and they'll see to it that your choice is presented in a "ready-to-prepare" state. So, now, onward to the inland waters and the sea! Do you have your boots and slicker? *OK, let's go.*

FILET OF SOLE MEUNIERE

1/2 cup (1 stick) butter	
1 to 1 1/2 pounds (4 filets) fresh Dover sole (or flounder)	
1/4 cup all-purpose flour	Salt to taste
Black Pepper to taste	Splash lemon juice
1 tablespoon fresh parsley, minced	6 lemon wedges

In a heavy skillet, heat half the butter over medium-low heat until it begins to brown just slightly. Dredge the fillets of sole in a mixture of the flour, salt and pepper, and gently add to the pan. Cook filets over very low heat for 5 minutes on each side or until the fish flakes. Be sure to use a large spatula or pancake turner to gently turn the fish to keep it from breaking apart. When cooked, remove the fillets to a platter and keep warm. Add the remaining butter to the pan, and again, slightly brown the butter; add a few splashes of lemon juice and parsley and heat thoroughly. Top the fish with the butter sauce and lemon wedges. Wonderful served with small whole parsley potatoes and spears of steamed broccoli.

Yield: 4 servings.

BAKED SALMON WITH MUSHROOMS

Non-stick cooking spray
4 to 6 half-pound fresh salmon filets (each about 1 inch thick)
1 tablespoon fresh parsley, chopped
1 tablespoon onion, minced
1 cup dry white wine
Salt to taste
Black pepper to taste
1/2 cup butter
2 tablespoons all-purpose flour
2 teaspoons lemon juice
4 tablespoons sour cream
4 ounces fresh white button mushrooms, whole

Preheat the oven to 400 degrees. Spray a medium baking dish with cooking spray; place the salmon filets in the baking dish, surrounded and covered with the onion, whole mushrooms, parsley, wine, salt and pepper. Cover and bake for 25 to 30 minutes or until fish flakes and is cooked (remove the cover during the last 10 minutes of cooking). Gently remove the fish filets to a platter (using a long spatula) and keep warm; reserve the mushrooms and keep warm. In a separate medium-size saucepan heat the butter over low heat; when melted, whisk in the flour and gradually adding the sauce from the baking dish. Blend and cook until smooth and thickened; stir in the lemon juice and the sour cream and continue cooking over very low heat while stirring for another 5 minutes. Top the fish with the reserved mushrooms and sauce. Delightful served with a dry white wine, perhaps a Sauvignon Blanc.
Yield: 4 to 6 servings.

SALMON WITH LEMON-GINGER SAUCE

6 tablespoons butter
2 tablespoons prepared and pureed chopped ginger

1 teaspoon garlic, minced	1 teaspoon fresh parsley, minced
1 tablespoon dry white wine	1 tablespoon lemon juice
2 tablespoons soy sauce	Salt to taste
Black pepper to taste	1 lemon, cut into wedges

2 1-inch-thick salmon filets, about 1/2 pound each

Preheat oven to 400 degrees. In a small saucepan, heat and blend the butter, ginger, garlic, parsley, wine, lemon juice, soy sauce, salt and pepper to taste. Place salmon in a greased shallow baking dish and baste generously with the prepared sauce. Bake uncovered for about 20 minutes or until salmon flakes easily; do not overcook. Remove fish to a serving platter or individual plates, using a long spatula. Top with any remaining sauce and garnish with lemon wedges.
Yield: 2 servings.

FINNAN HADDIE (HADDOCK)

2 pounds smoked haddock filets
2 tablespoons butter
Dash garlic powder
1 cup heavy cream (optional)
2 cups milk
1/4 cup fresh parsley, minced
1/2 teaspoon black pepper, coarsely ground

Originally from Scotland, this is now a very popular New England dish, often consumed on cold winter nights. It tends to be a bit salty, so soaking the fish in lukewarm water for 20 to 30 minutes prior to cooking will take care of the excess saltiness.

Place haddock filets in a large skillet, cover with milk and top with dots of butter, most of the parsley and sprinkles of garlic powder and pepper. Poach by bringing the milk ALMOST to a boil. Immediately lower heat to simmer, baste the fish, cover and cook until fish flakes (about 10 minutes). Our family used to serve this dish creamed. If that's your preference, continue as follows:

When fish is cooked, remove to a warm platter. Drain and reserve about 1 cup of the milk mix; return it to the skillet with 1 cup heavy cream. Adjust seasoning if necessary and return fish to the skillet to warm through. Again, remove fish to serving platter and top with remaining sauce and parsley. Wonderful served with boiled parsley potatoes and a green vegetable.

Yield: 4-plus servings.

BAKED TROUT AMANDINE

Non-stick cooking spray
4 tablespoons butter
1/2 cup onion, minced
8 ounces fresh white button mushrooms, sliced
1/2 cup blanched almonds, slivered
2 tablespoons fresh parsley, minced
1 cup dry white wine of choice
4 1-pound trout, dressed, heads and tails removed
Salt to taste
Black pepper to taste

Preheat the oven to 400 degrees. Spray a large but shallow glass casserole with cooking spray. In a skillet, melt butter and sauté the onion, mushrooms, almonds and parsley for 4 to 5 minutes. Add the wine and bring to a boil; then lower to simmer another few minutes. Arrange the trout in the casserole and top with the sauce; salt and pepper to taste. Bake loosely covered for about 25 to 30 minutes or until fish flakes easily. Remove to serve very hot. Goes nicely with herbed lemon asparagus, whole parsley potatoes and a chilled glass of Vouvray white wine.

Yield: 4 servings.

FISH CAKES

2 cups mashed potatoes, cooled
2 cups cooked cod, flaked
1 egg, beaten
1/4 cup fresh parsley, minced
Salt to taste
Black pepper to taste
1/2 cup virgin olive oil
1 egg, beaten with 1 tablespoon water
3/4 cup breadcrumbs

Here's another popular Friday night dinner in New England. It's simple and tasty, (even liked by those who are not "affishonados.")

In a medium mixing bowl, mix together the potatoes, fish, 1 beaten egg, parsley, salt and pepper. Shape the mix into 4 to 6 flat but chubby cakes. Heat the oil in a medium skillet over medium heat. Dip each cake into the SECOND egg wash, coat in the breadcrumbs, and gently drop into the skillet. Cook 4 or 5 minutes per side, until they're golden brown. Remove and drain on paper towels. Serve with tartar sauce and two sides of assorted vegetables.
Yield: 4 to 6 servings.

SCALLOPS WITH BROCCOLI

1 pound bay scallops, out of shell
1 cup dry white wine
2 tablespoons virgin olive oil
2 cups broccoli florets, blanched

1 tablespoon cornstarch
1 tablespoon soy sauce
1 small onion, minced
1/2 cup water

These tender small scallops are best if fresh; they're generally available in the fall and winter. Larger, frozen sea scallops are available year round, and are a second option.

Rinse scallops and place them in a large glass mixing bowl. In a separate bowl, whisk and blend the cornstarch, wine and soy sauce until smooth; pour wine mixture over the scallops. Stir and coat the bay scallops, then cover and let stand refrigerated for 10 to 15 minutes. In a large skillet over a medium-high flame, heat the olive oil, adding the onion and broccoli to stir-fry cook quickly. Lower heat to medium and add the scallops with their sauce; cook while tossing for about 5 minutes, adding a bit of water as needed to prevent sticking. If using larger sea scallops, a short amount of additional cooking time may be needed. Remember: bay scallops tend to be very delicate, so be careful not to overcook. A wonderful dish served with rice and a green veggie.
Yield: 4 servings.

MARYLAND CRAB CAKES à la AVERY

1 pound fresh, flaky crab meat
1 tablespoon fresh parsley, minced
2 tablespoons mayonnaise
Salt to taste
Breadcrumbs to bind
1 cup virgin olive oil

2 eggs, beaten
1 clove garlic, minced
1 tablespoon Dijon mustard
Black pepper to taste
Cracker crumbs to coat

In a mixing bowl, combine the crab with the eggs, parsley, and garlic and toss. Add the mayonnaise, mustard, salt and pepper and continue to mix; add just enough breadcrumbs to bind and form into 8 patties about 1/2-inch thick. Coat the patties with the cracker crumbs. Heat the oil in a large skillet to medium high, until a bit of bread sizzles when dropped in. Gently place the cakes in the skillet and cook 4 to 5 minutes per side, or until nicely browned. Remove cakes and drain on paper toweling. Serve with your choice of sauces (red, tartar, etc.) Nice as a light luncheon dish or as a main course.
Yield: 4 servings.

ALASKAN KING CRAB LEGS

2 to 4 12-ounce packages frozen Alaskan king crab legs
1 cup (2 sticks) butter, melted
1 tablespoon lemon juice
1 tablespoon fresh parsley, minced
1 clove garlic, minced

Packaged, frozen crab legs are always pre-cooked. Preheat oven to 400 degrees. Place frozen crab legs, flesh side up in a shallow baking dish. Blend butter, lemon juice, parsley and garlic and blend; brush the tops of the crab legs with the butter mixture and bake uncovered for 15 to 20 minutes until bubbly and thoroughly heated (remember to brush legs frequently during cooking with the butter mixture). Serve with your choice of side dishes.
Yield: 4 to 6 servings, depending on appetite.

LOBSTER NEWBURG

1 to 1 1/2 pounds cooked lobster meat, in small chunks
1/2 cup (1 stick) butter
1/2 cup brandy or dry vermouth
Heavy dash paprika
Dash nutmeg
Dash black pepper
Dash salt
1 tablespoon all-purpose flour
1 cup water
1 cup heavy cream

In a large skillet, sauté the lobster meat in melted butter over medium-high heat for 3 or 4 minutes. Add the brandy or vermouth, paprika, nutmeg, pepper and salt; simmer for another 3 or 4 minutes. In a small bowl, blend the flour and water; stir into the lobster mixture to slightly thicken. Add the cream and continue simmering another 2 to 4 minutes. Remove lobster from heat and set aside, but cover and keep warm. Serve over white rice or in pastry shells, accompanied by a fresh green veggie.
Yield: 4 to 6 servings.

BOILED LIVE MAINE LOBSTER

4 large, live Maine lobsters
(2 pounds each, shipped live and packed in seaweed)
    4 quarts water, salted with 4 tablespoons salt
    OR
    2 quarts salted water AND 2 quarts beer of choice (for a richer flavor)
Melted butter to taste
4 lemons, halved for garnish
4 ears fresh corn on the cob (optional)

In a very large kettle, bring your choice of liquid to a rolling boil. Using tongs, grab live lobsters by the back and (watch your hands now) plunge the little critters into the water (ignore the screams). Cover kettle and return to boil for approximately 12 minutes. Lobster is done when shell is bright red. Using tongs, remove lobsters and drain. Serve hot with melted butter and lemon and a side dish for collecting discarded shells. Shell crackers, lobster forks and bibs are highly recommended, although the mess is half the fun. If you must have a side dish, try boiled ears of corn. Add 4 prepared corn ears to about 4 quarts of UNSALTED boiling water for about 8 minutes and top dripping with butter.
Yield: 4 servings.

OYSTERS FLORENTINE CHAMPIGNON

1 10-ounce package frozen chopped spinach, cooked and
drained of excess liquid
Mushroom stems, (saved from the caps you'll be using) minced
Salt to taste
Black pepper to taste
24 extra-large fresh mushroom caps, rinsed, stems removed but saved
1/2 pound butter, softened
Non-stick cooking spray
Garlic powder to taste
24 oysters, shucked and drained
Parmesan cheese to taste

Preheat oven to 425 degrees. Mix the chopped spinach, minced mushroom stems and salt and pepper in a small bowl and hold aside. In a large skillet, sauté the mushroom caps in a bit of the butter over medium heat for about 3 minutes and remove from heat. Spray a shallow baking dish or sheet with non-stick cooking spray; arrange the mushroom caps (bottom cup side up) in the baking dish and fill each with a generous dollop of butter sprinkled with garlic powder, a bit of the spinach mix, and an oyster topped with cheese. Bake for approximately 5 to 7 minutes, until oyster starts to curl, and entire cap is heated through. Serve as a main course or as an appetizer on toast triangles. Yield: 4 entrée servings; 12 appetizer servings.

SHRIMP MEUNIERE

1 cup (2 sticks) butter
1 pound 30- to 40-count medium shrimp,
cooked, shelled, deveined and tails removed

1 cup milk	2 cups all-purpose flour
Salt to taste	Black pepper to taste
Lemon juice	1/2 cup fresh parsley, chopped very fine

Heat half the butter in a skillet over medium heat. Dip the cooked shrimp in milk, then dredge in the combination of the flour, salt and pepper, and sauté until heated through. Remove to heated platter, and drizzle with lemon juice. Add remaining butter and parsley to skillet and heat quickly until just starting to brown. Pour mix over the shrimp. Serve with potato au gratin and perhaps snow peas.
Yield: 5 to 6 servings (30 to 40 shrimp).

BAKED STUFFED NEW ENGLAND CLAMS

Rock salt
16 large hard-shell clams on half shell, minced
1/2 cup clam juice
1 1/2 cups fresh breadcrumbs, soft
1 clove garlic, minced (or to taste)
2 tablespoons onion, minced
1 tablespoon fresh parsley, minced
1 teaspoon lemon juice
Salt to taste
Black pepper to taste
Butter to line shells
3/4 cup seasoned breadcrumbs, dry
1/8 cup Parmesan cheese
4 tablespoons melted butter

The original Pilgrims loved them, and so do the latter-day Pilgrims. There are so many different types of clams, it can be a bit confusing. Suffice to say the best are from the East Coast (just ask any New Englander). It's your choice: the large hard-shell clams (such as those used in this recipe) were named Quahogs by the Indians and are best for stuffing. The mediums — better known as Cherrystones — are great steamed or on the half shell, and the tiny ones - or Littlenecks are best for eating on the half shell. The soft shell clams or Longnecks are best for steamers.

Preheat the oven to 400 degrees. Line the bed of a large but shallow baking pan with enough rock salt to support the clam shells firmly. Moisten the salt with a bit of sprayed water and heat in the oven for about 5 minutes; remove from oven. Mix the minced clams, clam juice, lemon juice, onion, parsley, garlic, salt and pepper with the soft breadcrumbs. Rinse and dry the clam shells and thoroughly rub with butter. Firmly seat the shells into the rock salt and spoon the clam mixture equally into the shells. Mix the SEASONED breadcrumbs, cheese and melted butter in a bowl. Top the filled shells with the seasoned crumbs and bake uncovered for 10 to 15 minutes. Tops should be nicely browned. Remove clams from rock salt to heated plates. Serve with creamed spinach and mashed potatoes.
Yield: 4 servings.

SHRIMP NEWBURG

4 tablespoons butter
Salt to taste
1/2 teaspoon nutmeg
2 egg yolks, beaten
1 pound small shrimp, cooked, deveined,
shelled and tails removed

4 tablespoons all-purpose flour
Black pepper to taste
1 1/2 cups heavy cream
1/2 cup dry sherry

Melt the butter over low heat in a skillet and whisk in flour, salt, pepper and nutmeg until blended. Add the cream, stirring constantly until smooth and beginning to thicken. In a separate bowl, slowly whisk a bit of this sauce into the egg yolks; pour the egg-sauce mixture back into the skillet and continue whisking to blend. Add the shrimp and heat through, about 5 minutes, stirring occasionally. When thoroughly heated, stir in the sherry and serve over a rice dish of your choice. Yield: 4 servings.

FROG LEGS PROVENCALE

2 pounds frog legs, rinsed and well dried
1/2 cup milk
2 cloves garlic, minced
3 tomatoes, seeded, finely chopped
1/2 cup dry red wine
Black pepper to taste

1/2 cup dry white wine
2 medium onions, minced
1/4 cup olive oil
1/2 teaspoon sugar
Salt to taste
1/2 cup fresh parsley, minced

When most people think of frog legs, the image of that cute little toad ("Ribbit, ribbit!") comes to mind. Truth be known, frog legs are delicious and available year round. When cooking, prepare about 2 to 3 "sets" per serving. Purchase frog legs that are pale pink, very fresh and ready to cook. For the uninitiated, the flavor and texture of frog legs are comparable to chicken.

In a large fry pan (do NOT use an iron skillet), poach the frog legs in just enough liquid, equal parts white wine and milk, to cover them. Cover skillet and simmer for 15 minutes or until thoroughly cooked. Remove legs to a serving dish, cover and keep warm. In a separate skillet, sauté onion and garlic in the olive oil until golden, about 5 to 10 minutes. Add the tomatoes, sugar and red wine to the onion mixture and heat thoroughly (about 5 minutes longer). Pour onion mixture over the frog legs to coat. Season with salt and pepper to taste and top with the parsley before serving. Yield: 4 or more servings.

SAUCES&GRAVIES:
dripping with satisfaction

"A man's doubts and fears are his worst enemy."
—William Wrigley, Jr

A short chapter this shall be, to give you the technique and preparation of some of the more popular sauces and gravies to complement many of the meats and recipes in this volume. These are often the coup de grace for a well-prepared meal.

There are many very good pre-packaged sauces and gravies on the market, should you not feel daring. However, for the adventurers in the crowd, let's try some of these:

PARSLEY WHITE SAUCE

4 tablespoons butter
4 tablespoons all-purpose flour
2 cups milk
4 tablespoons fresh parsley, minced
Salt to taste
Black pepper to taste

This sauce goes nicely with fish dishes! Note the following recipes for some tasty variations.

In a skillet (do NOT use aluminum with white sauces), melt the butter over low heat. Make a paste by blending in the flour and stirring constantly. Continue to stir and add the milk slowly until sauce is smooth. Add parsley, salt and pepper, cover and take from the heat for a few minutes. Serve with your favorite dish.
Yield: about 2 cups.

WHITE MUSHROOM SAUCE

1/4 pound fresh mushrooms, buttons or sliced
1 clove garlic, minced
1/4 cup onion, minced
2 tablespoons virgin olive oil

Gently sauté the mushrooms, garlic and onion in olive oil until onion is tender and glassy. Add onion mixture to Parsley White Sauce (see previous recipe) for a terrific variation.
Yield: about 2 cups.

MUSTARD SAUCE

1/2 cup Dijon mustard
2 teaspoons wine vinegar

This tangy sauce is great with pork dishes!

Add these ingredients to the basic Parsley White Sauce and warm over low heat. Cover and remove from heat; let set for a few minutes and serve.
Yield: about 2 to 3 cups.

MINT SAUCE

2 tablespoons fresh mint, minced

To the previously listed Parsley White Sauce recipe, substitute mint for parsley. Cover and let set for about 5 minutes before serving.
Yield: about 2 cups.

PAN GRAVY

1 cup beef broth
1 cup water
1/2 cup reserved meat drippings
2 tablespoons pre-sifted flour
Additional water as needed
Gravy master (optional)
Salt to taste
Black pepper to taste

This gravy is great on its own, or you can try the variation listed in the following recipe.

Drain drippings from roast pan, holding about 1/2 cup in reserve. Add the beef broth and 1 cup water to the pan, heating over low heat while stirring and scraping bits from the bottom of the pan. Transfer broth-drippings mixture to a skillet and blend in the flour, stirring constantly over medium heat. Add additional water if necessary and continue to stir to desired consistency. Add Gravy Master browner if you wish. Season with salt and pepper to taste.
Yield: about 2 cups.

CAPER-LEMON SAUCE

1 cup mayonnaise
2 tablespoons fresh parsley, minced
2 tablespoons capers, minced
4 tablespoons lemon juice

This sauce is an ideal seafood accompaniment.

Blend mayonnaise with all the ingredients.
Yield: 1 to 1 1/2 cups.

MUSHROOM GRAVY

1/4 to 1/2 pound fresh mushrooms, sliced
1 small onion, minced
2 tablespoons virgin olive oil

Sauté the mushrooms and minced onion in oil for about 5 minutes, before adding to the Pan Gravy (see previous recipe). Cover the gravy and simmer over very low heat for another 5 minutes. Add additional seasonings as needed.
Yield: about 2 to 3 cups.

LEMON SAUCE

2 cups vegetable broth
1 tablespoon cornstarch
2 tablespoons water
1/4 cup butter
1 egg yolk, beaten
3 to 4 tablespoons lemon juice
1 tablespoon fresh parsley, minced
Salt to taste
Black pepper to taste

This sauce is nice with fish or veal.

In a medium saucepan, heat the vegetable broth. Blend cornstarch with water and mix into the broth, stirring constantly. When sauce begins to thicken, add the butter and blend it in thoroughly. Reduce heat to low, cover and simmer for a few minutes. In a separate dish, blend a bit of the sauce with the egg, then return it all to the pan with the lemon juice and continue heating while stirring for another few minutes. Remove from heat; add parsley, salt and pepper to taste.
Yield: about 2 cups.

GARLIC SAUCE

1 1/2 cups beef stock
2 bay leaves
1 1/2 cups water
2 cloves garlic, minced (more to taste)
1 onion, minced
1/3 teaspoon celery salt
1/4 teaspoon black pepper
1/2 cup heavy cream
Lemon slices
Mint leaves

This sauce goes nicely with lamb.

Combine beef stock, bay leaves, water, garlic, onion, salt and pepper in a medium skillet and simmer covered over low heat for 15 to 20 minutes. Strain out the solid residue pouring liquid into a clean pan. Add cream, heating and stirring uncovered for 5 minutes over very low heat. Top with sliced lemon and mint leaves.
Yield: about 3 cups.

CHEESE SAUCE
1 1/2 cups Cheddar cheese, grated
1/2 teaspoon Dijon mustard
1/2 clove garlic, minced

Add these ingredients to the basic Parsley White Sauce recipe. Add more milk as needed and stir until blended and heated through.
Yield: about 3 cups.

BRANDY SAUCE
1/2 cup granulated sugar
2 tablespoons cornstarch
2 cups milk
1/2 cup brandy
1/4 cup butter, softened
1/4 cup raisins
1/2 teaspoon almond extract
Pinch cinnamon

In a medium saucepan, blend sugar and cornstarch while adding milk slowly over medium heat. Add brandy and continue to stir until mix comes to a boil. Reduce heat to low and simmer uncovered for just a few minutes, while stirring occasionally. Add the butter, raisins, almond and cinnamon and stir until well blended. Nice served over warm bread pudding.
Yield: 2 1/2 cups.

VANILLA BANANA SAUCE
1/2 cup granulated sugar
2 tablespoons cornstarch
2 cups light cream
1/4 cup butter, softened
1 teaspoon vanilla extract
1 teaspoon banana extract
Pinch of nutmeg

Blend sugar and cornstarch in a saucepan over medium heat, while slowly adding cream. Stir continuously; bring just to a boil. Reduce heat to simmer uncovered for another few minutes while stirring occasionally. Add the butter, vanilla extract, banana extract and nutmeg and stir until blended. Remove from heat and serve over your favorite pudding, ice cream or other dessert.
Yield: 2 1/2 cups.

STRAWBERRY SAUCE
1/2 cup granulated sugar
1 tablespoons cornstarch
2 tablespoons water
1/2 cup apple jelly
2 10-ounce packages frozen, crushed strawberries

Blend sugar, cornstarch and water in a saucepan over medium heat, stirring continuously. Add apple jelly and continue to heat. Add crushed strawberries and continue to heat through over low heat. Try this over ice cream or sponge cake.
Yield: 1 to 1 1/2 cups.

DESSERTS & QUICK BREADS: decadent pleasures

"Remember, optimism is essential to achievement, and it is also the foundation of courage and true progress."
—Nicholas Murray Butler

Many Americans have a "sweet tooth," and a bit of sweet at the end of a meal is a pleasant and relaxing way to end it.

There are many directions in which to go when classifying desserts, so we shall cover but a few, leaving your imaginations to flourish. What we must try to remember is that a little dessert goes a long way; it isn't meant to be another meal. So, if you're ready, let's have a go at a few of them.

CRANBERRY FRUIT SHERBET

1 quart 2 percent milk
1 16-ounce can frozen cranberry juice concentrate
1/4 cup sugar

This dessert is light, easy to prepare and absolutely delicious. Should you prefer something other than cranberry, you can use any fruit juice concentrate (consider apple, orange, lime, lemon or papaya).

In a large bowl, use an electric mixer on the low setting to thoroughly blend milk and fruit concentrate; gradually add the sugar. When thoroughly mixed, pour into a covered, freezer-safe container and put in the freezer. After about 2 hours, stir the sherbet and return to the freezer until completely frozen. *Voilà! Was this easy, or what?*
Yield: About 1 quart.

BAKED BANANAS

4 bananas, not quite ripe, peeled
1/4 cup butter, melted
1/2 cup dark-brown sugar
4 orange wheels, halved
Grand Marnier liqueur

Preheat oven to 350 degrees. Split bananas lengthwise, and place in a shallow glass casserole; top with melted butter. Sprinkle with sugar and bake for 15 minutes until bananas are soft. Place 2 banana slices on each dessert dish with an orange slice wedged between the bananas. Drizzle with Grand Marnier and serve.
Yield: 4 servings.

APRICOT APPLESAUCE

3 pounds Jonathan or Granny Smith apples, halved, cored, peeled and cut into chunks
1 cup dried apricots, cut in quarters
1/4 cup raisins
1 cup sugar
1 1/2 cups water (enough to cover)

Combine all ingredients in a large saucepan and simmer uncovered over low heat for 25 to 30 minutes, until apples are very soft. Lightly mash the sauce if preferred. Remove from heat Sauce may be served warm or chilled.
Yield: 6 servings.

BERRIES GRAND MARNIER

1 quart raspberries or strawberries, stemmed and washed
(If strawberries are large, they should be halved.)
2 tablespoons granulated sugar
1/2 cup Grand Marnier liqueur
1 cup whipped cream

Sprinkle the berries with sugar and toss lightly; let berries stand at room temperature for 10 to 15 minutes. Cover with the Grand Marnier and toss again. Cover and chill 3 to 4 hours before serving, remembering to toss the berries frequently. Serve in individual dessert dishes and top with whipped cream.
Yield: 4 servings.

PEARS MELBA FRAISES

Pears

1 cup water
1 cup sugar
3 Anjou pears, halved, cored and peeled
2 tablespoons lemon juice
1 to 2 pints of vanilla or strawberry ice cream

Melba Sauce

1 pint fresh strawberries
(or 2 10-ounce packages thawed frozen strawberries)
1 tablespoon cornstarch   2 tablespoons water
1/4 cup apple jelly   1/2 cup sugar

Top With

Splash of Grand Marnier liqueur (optional)

In a medium skillet, mix water and sugar and bring to a boil over medium heat, stirring until dissolved; continue boiling for another minute. Add pears and reduce heat to simmer uncovered for 15 minutes until pears are tender, occasionally basting pears with the sugar sauce. Add lemon juice to the sugar sauce, and remove from the heat to cool. When ready to serve, spoon ice cream into dessert dishes, place one pear half on top of each with the hollow side down. Top with Melba Sauce and Grand Marnier (optional).

To make sauce: Puree strawberries in a blender. Mix cornstarch and water in a small bowl. In a small saucepan, cook strawberries, the water-cornstarch mixture, sugar and jelly. Cook over medium heat until thickened.
Yield: 6 servings.

BAKED APPLES

4 large Delicious or Rome Apples
4 tablespoons butter
1 snack-size box raisins (1 1/2 to 2 ounces)
1 cup water
1/4 teaspoon nutmeg

4 bread rounds

1 cup dark-brown sugar
1/4 teaspoon ground cinnamon
1 cup heavy cream

Preheat oven to 350 degrees. Core apples and peel away the skin around the top inch of each apple. Place the apples atop the bread rounds in a shallow, ungreased baking dish. Place one tablespoon butter, raisins and a bit of the brown sugar in each apple. In a saucepan, mix and heat the water, the rest of the brown sugar, cinnamon and nutmeg. Boil sugar mixture for 5 minutes; remove from heat and pour a bit of the sugar mixture over each of the apples. Bake apples uncovered for 1 hour or until they are tender (baste apples with the remaining syrup during baking). Serve apples on individual dessert dishes and drizzle with heavy cream.
Yield: 4 servings.

SOUFFLE à la ORANGE

Butter to prepare soufflé dishes
6 eggs, yolks and whites separated
1/3 cup + 3 tablespoons granulated sugar
2 tablespoons orange zest
1/2 cup orange juice with pulp
1 tablespoon Grand Marnier liqueur
Confectioner's sugar

This recipe will take a bit of planning, but it's a great dessert for special occasions. You'll need four 1 1/4 cup soufflé dishes, which can be found really inexpensively in "dollar stores" or even your market. So, are you game? Yes? Great, let's go.

Preheat the oven to 350 degrees. Coat the insides of soufflé dishes with butter and use 1 tablespoon granulated sugar to sprinkle inside the four dishes. Place the separated egg yolks in a bowl; add 1/3 cup granulated sugar, zest, juice and liqueur. Using a wire whip, beat briskly until well blended. In another bowl, use a wire whip to beat egg whites with remaining 2 tablespoons of granulated sugar until the egg whites are stiff. Gently but rapidly fold (don't whip) the yolk mixture into the whites until well blended. Spoon equal amounts of the mix into the soufflé dishes. Place soufflé dishes on a cookie sheet and bake for 12 to 15 minutes. Dust with the confectioner's sugar and serve immediately (perhaps with just another drizzle of Grand Marnier) and coffee.
An international delight. That wasn't so difficult, was it?
Yield: 4 servings.

DR PEPPER PRALINES

1 cup granulated sugar
1 cup dark brown sugar
1 cup Dr Pepper soft drink
1 cup miniature marshmallows
2/3 cup pecans, chopped

Using a candy thermometer and over low heat, blend the sugars and Dr Pepper, being sure to **STIR CONSTANTLY.** Gradually heat mixture to soft ball stage (a temperature of 240 degrees). Remove the mix from the heat and stir in the marshmallows and pecans. Mix well until the marshmallows dissolve. Quickly drop onto waxed paper a tablespoon at a time; cool. Serve in place of after-dinner mints or as a mid-evening sweet snack.
Yield: 24 pralines.

BAKED INDIAN PUDDING

1 quart milk
1/4 cup cornmeal
1 cup dark molasses
1/3 cup packed dark brown sugar
1/2 cup raisins
1/2 cup butter
1/4 teaspoon salt
1/2 teaspoon ground ginger
1/2 teaspoon cinnamon
Non-stick cooking spray

Preheat the oven to 325 degrees. Mix 1 cup of the milk and the cornmeal until blended. In the top of a double boiler, heat another 2 cups of the milk; simmer until the mixture steams. Mix in the cornmeal blend, and cook for 20 minutes while stirring occasionally. Stir in the molasses and brown sugar, and cook for another 3 or 4 minutes; remove from the heat. Mix in the raisins, butter, salt, ginger and cinnamon. Pour the mixture into a 1- or 2-quart baking dish sprayed with cooking spray, and gently pour remaining 1 cup milk over the mixture. Bake uncovered 1 1/2 hours. Serve warm with whipped cream or French vanilla ice cream.
Yield: 6 servings *(or 2 if I'm included!)*

STRAWBERRY-CRUMB APPLE PIE

1 1/4 cups granulated sugar
1/4 cup all-purpose flour
1/4 teaspoon salt
2 cups fresh strawberries, crushed
1/8 cup water
1/2 teaspoon almond extract
6 Granny Smith apples, cored, peeled, sliced
1 9-inch uncooked, prepared pie shell
1/2 cup blanched almonds, crushed
1 cup breadcrumbs, plain
1/4 cup dark brown sugar
1/4 cup melted butter

Preheat oven to 375 degrees. In a medium-large saucepan, blend granulated sugar, 1/4 cup flour and salt. Add strawberries, water and almond extract, and blend together over medium-high heat, stirring continuously. When mixture begins to boil, immediately lower heat and simmer covered for 4 to 6 minutes, stirring occasionally. Stir in sliced apples and continue to simmer covered for another 3 or 4 minutes or until apples are tender. Pour the mix into the pie shell and set aside. In a separate bowl, mix almonds, breadcrumbs, 3/4 cup flour, brown sugar and butter until well blended. Use crumb-nut mixture to top pie. Bake 30 minutes.
Yield: 8 servings.

ALMOND-CARROT PIE

1 pound carrots, washed, tips and tops removed
1/4 cup orange honey
5 tablespoons butter, softened
2 teaspoons cinnamon
1/2 teaspoon almond extract
1/2 cup dark brown sugar
2 eggs
1/2 teaspoon salt
1 teaspoon vanilla extract
1/2 cup blanched almonds, chopped
1/2 cup granulated sugar
1 9-inch uncooked, deep-dish prepared pie shell

Preheat oven to 350 degrees. In a steamer, steam the carrots until just barely cooked. Immediately remove from the heat and cool for 5 minutes. Place the carrots in a food processor and puree until smooth. Add the orange honey, eggs, butter, salt, cinnamon, vanilla extract, almond extract and almonds; continue to blend until smooth. Move this mix into a large bowl. In a separate bowl, mix together the two sugars. Gently fold the sugars into the carrot mixture until well blended. Pour mixture into the pie shell and bake for about 1 hour. Pie will be done when an inserted toothpick comes out clean.
Yield: 8 servings.

CHOCOLATE CHEESECAKE

1/2 cup walnuts, chopped
1 9-inch prepared crumb pie crust (preferably chocolate)
9 ounces cream cheese, softened
3/4 cup sour cream
1 1/2 cup whole milk
1 4-ounce package instant chocolate pudding mix
1 pound fresh whole strawberries, washed and hulled

Sprinkle the nuts into the pie crust. Next, combine the cream cheese, sour cream and milk into a blender; blend well. Add the pudding mix and blend again for 30 seconds until smooth. Pour chocolate mixture into the pie crust and top with fresh strawberries, top-side down. Loosely cover and chill until well set.

Yield: 10 or 12 servings *(depending upon how many are chocoholics!)*

CARROT BREAD

3/4 cup granulated sugar
1/2 cup packed light brown sugar
3/4 cup virgin olive oil
2 cups all-purpose flour
2 teaspoons baking powder
1 teaspoon baking soda
1 teaspoon cinnamon
1 teaspoon nutmeg
Dash ground clove
Dash salt
2 eggs, beaten
1 1/2 cups fresh grated carrots
1/2 cup pine nuts
1/2 teaspoon vanilla extract
1/8 teaspoon almond extract

Preheat the oven to 350 degrees. Grease and flour a 5-by-9-inch loaf pan. In a large bowl, mix together sugars and oil. Sift flour, baking powder, baking soda, cinnamon, nutmeg, clove and salt into the bowl, while continuing to stir. In a separate dish, beat the eggs. Stir eggs into the large bowl and mix until thoroughly blended. Add carrots, nuts, vanilla and almond, and thoroughly mix. Pour batter into the loaf pan and bake for 1 hour or until a toothpick inserted into the bread comes out clean. Let bread cool in the pan for 15 minutes, and then turn out onto a wire rack to cool completely. Wrap in plastic wrap to ensure freshness.

Yield: 1 loaf, about 12 servings.

SPICE WALNUT CAKE
Cake

        2 cups all-purpose flour + flour for dusting cake pan
        1/4 cup cornstarch
        1 cup granulated sugar
        1 teaspoon baking powder
        3/4 teaspoon baking soda
        1 teaspoon salt
        3/4 teaspoon cinnamon
        3/4 teaspoon nutmeg
        3/4 cup shortening
        1 cup heavy cream
        3 large eggs, beaten

Frosting

        1 3-ounce package cream cheese, softened
        1/3 cup butter, softened
        3/4 teaspoon ground cinnamon
        4 cups confectioners' sugar
        1 teaspoon vanilla extract
        2 tablespoons milk
        1/4 cup walnuts, crushed

Preheat the oven to 350 degrees. Grease two 9-inch round cake pans and dust with flour. In a medium-large bowl using a sifter, sift together the flour, cornstarch, sugar, baking powder, baking soda, salt, cinnamon and nutmeg. Add the shortening and cream and blend with a hand mixer for 2 minutes. Add the eggs and continue to beat for another 1 to 2 minutes until blended. Pour the mixture into the cake pans and bake for 30 minutes or until a toothpick inserted into the cake comes out clean and indicates it's done. Remove cake from the oven to cool in pans for 10 minutes; turn cakes out onto wire racks to thoroughly cool. Prepare this frosting or use a canned frosting of your choice.

While cake is baking, prepare the frosting as follows:
In a medium bowl, blend together cream cheese, butter and cinnamon. Slowly add the sugar, blending until thoroughly mixed. Stir in the vanilla extract, and gradually add the milk until spreading consistency is reached. Frost one layer; place second layer on top and ice second layer. Top frosted cake with crushed walnuts.
Yield: 6 to 8 servings.

COLA CAKE WITH PEANUT BUTTER FROSTING

Cake

> Non-stick cooking spray
> 2 cups all-purpose flour
> 2 cups sugar
> 1/2 pound butter
> 1 cup cola
> 2 tablespoons unsweetened cocoa
> 1/2 cup buttermilk
> 2 eggs, well beaten
> 1 teaspoon baking soda
> 1 teaspoon vanilla extract
> 1 1/2 cups miniature marshmallows

Frosting

> 6 tablespoons butter
> 1 cup packed light brown sugar
> 2/3 cup creamy peanut butter
> 1/4 cup milk
> 2/3 cup chopped nuts of choice (optional)

Preheat oven to 350 degrees. Spray a 2-by-9-by-13-inch baking pan with cooking spray and use just a bit of the flour to coat the pan. In a large mixing bowl, combine remaining flour with sugar. Melt the butter; add cola and cocoa and stir until blended. Add cola mixture to the flour mixture and stir until blended. Add buttermilk, eggs, baking soda and vanilla, and continue to mix well. Stir in the marshmallows; pour the mix into the prepared cake pan. Bake for 40 minutes or until a toothpick inserted in the cake comes out clean. Remove the cake and frost while still warm.

While cake is baking, prepare the frosting as follows:
Cream together the butter, sugar and peanut butter; add the milk and stir well. Add nuts if desired. Spread frosting over warm cake. Place the frosted cake about 4 inches under a preheated broiler for A FEW SECONDS until frosting starts to bubble. (Make sure it doesn't burn!) Let the cake sit for an hour before slicing.
Talk about delicious!
Yield: About 12 servings.

BANANA-ALMOND BREAD

2/3 cup raisins
1/3 cup brandy
3 bananas, mashed
3/4 cup packed light brown sugar
1/3 cup olive oil
2 eggs, beaten
3/4 cup Wondra quick-mix flour
1 teaspoon baking soda
1 teaspoon baking powder
1 teaspoon salt
1 teaspoon ground allspice
1/2 cup chopped toasted almonds
1 teaspoon almond extract

Preheat the oven to 350 degrees. Grease and flour a 5-by-9-inch loaf pan. Combine the raisins, almond extract and brandy in a small saucepan and bring to simmer over medium-low heat. Remove from the heat and set aside to cool for 15 minutes. In a mixing bowl, blend bananas, sugar, oil and eggs using an electric mixer for just a minute or so. Sift the flour, baking soda, baking powder, salt and allspice together into the batter; mix with a large wooden spoon until blended. Lastly, add the almonds and the brandied raisins and gently stir in. Pour the mix into the loaf pan and bake for one hour or until a toothpick inserted into the bread comes out clean. Allow the bread to cool in the pan for 15 minutes, and then turn out onto a wire rack to cool completely. Wrap in plastic wrap to ensure freshness.
Yield: 1 loaf, about 12 servings.

BREAD PUDDING

Pudding

      4 cups white bread, day old or stale,
      cut into 1-inch cubes
      1 cup raisins
      4 cups milk, slightly warmed
      4 eggs, beaten
      1/2 cup granulated sugar
      1 tablespoon butter, softened
      1/2 teaspoon salt
      1 teaspoon vanilla extract

Sauce

      1 cup sugar
      1/2 cup butter, softened
      1/2 cup heavy cream
      1 teaspoon vanilla

Preheat the oven to 350 degrees. Butter a 2-quart casserole dish. In a large bowl, toss together the bread cubes and raisins and soak in 1 cup of the milk for just a few minutes; then move to the casserole dish. In a separate bowl, beat together the eggs and 1/2 cup sugar; add the remaining 3 cups milk, 1 tablespoon butter, salt and vanilla extract and continue to mix until blended. Pour egg mixture over the bread cubes and stir gently, making sure bread is covered. Place the casserole in a larger roasting pan; pour HOT water into the roaster, about half way up the sides of the casserole dish. Bake 1 hour. Check for doneness by inserting a knife in the center of the pudding; when it comes out clean, the pudding is done. This pudding may be served cool or hot, and with or without the sauce.

To prepare the sauce: mix sugar, butter, heavy cream and vanilla in a small saucepan over medium-high heat, stirring until it comes to a boil. Reduce heat to simmer and continue to stir for a few more minutes. A nice sauce, especially when served with warm pudding. Yield: 6 to 9 servings.

BLUEBERRY-ALMOND MUFFINS

Non-stick cooking spray
2 cups all-purpose flour
1/2 teaspoon salt
1 cup blueberries, fresh, rinsed and dried
1 cup milk
1/3 cup virgin olive oil

1/4 cup sugar
1 tablespoon baking powder

1 egg, beaten
1/2 cup almonds, chopped

A great treat for breakfast or dessert.
Preheat oven to 400 degrees. Coat a 12-cup muffin pan with non-stick cooking spray or use paper muffin inserts in each well. In a medium mixing bowl, sift together flour, sugar, salt and baking powder. Make a well (or indentation) in the center of the sifted mix. In another bowl, mix blueberries, milk, beaten egg, oil and almonds and pour into the center of the dry mix. Combine the dry and liquid ingredients until the batter is moist—be careful not to over-mix. Fill the cups 2/3 full with batter and bake 15 to 20 minutes until muffins are golden. Use the toothpick trick to see if they're done; insert a toothpick in the center of the muffin. If it comes out clean, they're done.
Yield: 12 muffins.

BANANA-RAISIN MUFFINS

1/4 pound butter
2 to 3 very ripe bananas, mashed (about 2 cups)
3/4 cup raisins
3/4 cup dark brown sugar, packed
2 eggs, beaten
1 teaspoon baking soda
1 tablespoon baking powder
1/2 teaspoon nutmeg
1 cup heavy cream

2 cups cake flour
1/2 teaspoon ground cinnamon
1/2 teaspoon salt

Preheat oven to 375 degrees. Melt butter in a small saucepan; remove from heat and set aside. Place paper liners in one 16-cup or two 8-cup muffin tins. In a large mixing bowl, blend together bananas, butter, cream, raisins, brown sugar and eggs. In a separate mixing bowl, blend baking soda, flour, baking powder, cinnamon, nutmeg and salt. Fold the dry ingredients into the banana mix until just blended. Spoon the mix into the muffin cups until full, and bake for 20 minutes. Transfer the muffins to a cooling rack.
Yield: 16 muffins.

BEVERAGES: running hot&cold

"Thank you for your coffee, Signior.
I shall miss that when we leave Casablanca!"
—Ingrid Bergman in *Casablanca*

When beverages are mentioned, we could be talking about everything from chilled vodka to an after-dinner cordial to the immense variety of coffees and teas.

In no way are we going to try to cover all drinks; what we would like to do is present a bit of variety to start or top off any wonderful meal you may have prepared. Who knows? Perhaps you'll invent something new to add to the list; after all, someone has to do it. Cheers!

(Unless otherwise noted, all yields listed within this chapter are for single servings.)

COFFEES

Many think that coffee started with the Turks, when actually it started with the Arab Muslims and then the Turks. As they invaded Europe, they brought their coffee with them. Then, thanks to the thoughtful Colonists, coffee made its way to what's now the United States.

Great coffees now abound all over the world — in exotic spots like Java (hence the colloquialism), Colombia, Jamaica, Brazil and Hawaii. So as you begin to experiment with coffee drinks, consider trying a new blend or variation.

Some of the more traditional, non-alcoholic coffee drinks are:

ESPRESSO

If you don't happen to have an espresso machine, they're readily available in many stores, some more elaborate than others. For the average couple, a small inexpensive machine will do and can nicely prepare a couple of cups at a time. Espresso is a strong coffee, made by steam passing through the coffee grounds under pressure, and is particularly favored as an after-dinner treat. Simply follow the directions! If you prefer, espresso pots are also available; while they are not the same as espresso machines, the coffee they make is very similar.

DEMITASSE

Demitasse is quite simply very strong French or Italian roast coffee served in very small "demitasse" cups. Looked on fondly by those who like strong coffee, but not espresso.

CAFÉ AU LAIT

This is the most traditional of European breakfast coffees and is prepared by brewing an equal amount of demitasse and scalded milk, and then filling cups simultaneously with both.

CAPPUCCINO

This variation is simply prepared by mixing espresso and hot milk in cappuccino cups (sized midway between a demitasse and regular cup) and sprinkling with cinnamon or adding a cinnamon stick.

COFFEE VIENNA

This drink is created by mixing hot, strong coffee with an equal amount of hot milk and topping with whipped cream. Not showy, but delicious.

MOCHA COFFEE

Blend equal amounts of hot chocolate and demitasse; very similar to cafe au lait.

Some popular alcoholic coffee drinks include:

CAFÉ ROYALE

This is basically a demitasse with a bit of cognac. Prepare a cup; then place a sugar cube covered with a splash of cognac on a spoon, and light it; when the sugar is melted and fire dies out, add to the coffee. A nice touch!

CAFÉ DIABLE

For a great presentation of coffee after that dinner party for 6, do the following: Hopefully you'll have a chafing dish (to take full advantage of the show) if not, use a large, fairly deep saucepan. Place 6 to 8 whole cloves, a stick of cinnamon, 6 sugar cubes, and a few strips of lemon rind in the dish or pan. Add 1/2 cup cognac or brandy and ignite it, stirring as the flames go out. Add a quart of hot coffee (preferably strong) and continue heating for another minute or two. Pour into individual cups and serve.

Yield: 6 servings.

TEAS

All teas fit into one of three basic categories:

BLACK

Most of these come from India, and are quite fragrant, including the delicate Darjeeling from the Himalayas; the Earl Grey blend from Taiwan, and the English Breakfast teas, a blend of mellow teas from Sri Lanka and India.

GREEN

Most green teas come from Japan and China. You'll find them served in Asian restaurants.

OOLONG

These teas also are from the Orient, most often Taiwan. The most popular of the Oolong teas is the lovely and mild Formosa Oolong.

TEA-LIKE BEVERAGES

Many tea-like beverages, or what are known as tisanes, started in Colonial times, and are still available today, such as those known as: sassafras tea, rose hips tea, chamomile tea and peppermint tea. For convenience, buy them in tea bag form, readily available in your supermarket.

HOT TEA

The ideal way to prepare teas is to use a porcelain teapot. Pour boiling water into the pot and swish it around to heat the pot; then dump that water. Put one teaspoon of tea or 1 teabag into the heated pot for each cup, and add 1 cup of boiling water for each cup you want to make. Cover and let steep (brew) for about 4 minutes or desired strength is reached. Serve tea with your choice of lemon or sugar, and milk if you prefer. For a pleasant additional flavor to your tea, you may consider adding a few whole cloves or sticks of cinnamon to the brewing process. Remember, when using loose tea, you'll have to pour tea through a strainer to serve.

ICED TEA

To make iced tea, prepare teas as noted for hot tea, but add an additional tea bag into the pot, so the tea is much stronger. Then fill tall 12-ounce glasses with ice cubes and slowly pour hot tea into the glasses, adding more ice as needed. Garnish with a sprig of mint perhaps and a wheel of lemon and/or sugar to taste.

CITRUS TEA

To your hot tea preparation, add 1 whole clove and 1/2 teaspoon of orange juice per cup prepared. Garnish with lemon or sugar and a stick of cinnamon. Serve hot or iced.

MILK

The beauty of this beverage is that it can be prepared in so many ways—in shakes, sodas, nogs, cocoas, floats, frappes or plain and icy cold.

When heating milk, always remember to heat slowly over low flame, and do not bring it to a boil. If a recipe calls for "scalded" milk, heat milk just until bubbles form around the edges. If you're worried about your waistline, use skimmed milk—not bad on its own and virtually the same taste as whole milk when used in other recipes. Following are some wonderful milk drinks that can be topped with an endless variety of garnish, such as: whipped cream, cinnamon, nutmeg, marshmallows or peppermint—just remember to garnish with something appropriate to the drink you're preparing.

HOT COCOA

Mix 1 tablespoon each of cocoa and sugar in a sauce pan, slowly stirring in 1/3 cup of water. Bring to a slow boil over low heat, stirring constantly for a couple of minutes. Add 2/3 cup of milk, and continue to warm until heated through but not boiling.

BUTTERSCOTCH MILK

Add 2 tablespoons of butterscotch and a dash of vanilla extract to a 12-ounce glass of cold milk and stir. Top with a bit of shaved dark chocolate.

CHOCOLATE MILK

Add 3 tablespoons of chocolate syrup and a dash of vanilla extract to a 12-ounce glass of cold milk and stir. Top with whipped cream and a cinnamon stick.

MALTED MILK

Add 2 tablespoons of chocolate malted milk powder and a dash of vanilla extract to a 12-ounce glass of milk and stir very well. Top with whipped cream and dark chocolate shavings.

MOCHA MILK

Blend 1 teaspoon of instant coffee with a bit of warm water and add with 1 tablespoon of chocolate syrup and a dash of vanilla extract to a 12-ounce glass of milk. Top with whipped cream and a dash of nutmeg.

MILKSHAKES, SODAS, FLOATS & FRAPPES

It's been many years since my days as a soda "jerk," but memories of these drinks come rushing back as if it were yesterday. With the advent of the blender, the making of a milk shake or blended drinks became a breeze. Here are a few recipes for your consideration. For a FRAPPE (sometimes known as a frosty), add a scoop of ice cream into the blender. For a FLOAT, leave a bit of room at the top of the shake for a scoop of ice cream.

COFFEE MILKSHAKE

Add 2 teaspoons of instant coffee and 2 teaspoons sugar to 1 1/2 cups cold milk and blend for a few seconds.

CHOCOLATE MILKSHAKE

Add 3 tablespoons of chocolate syrup and dash of vanilla extract to 1 1/2 cups cold milk and blend for a few seconds.

STRAWBERRY MILKSHAKE

Add 3 tablespoons of strawberry sauce or syrup to 1 1/2 cups cold milk and blend for a few seconds. If making a float, top with a fresh strawberry.

VANILLA MILKSHAKE

Add 2 tablespoons of vanilla extract to 1 1/2 cups cold milk and blend for a few seconds. To make this an orange-vanilla shake, add 1/4 cup of orange juice before blending. If making a float, top with a wheel of fresh orange.

ICE CREAM SODA

Boy, did I make a lot of these in my "jerk" days! For the basic soda, add 1/4 cup very cold milk to a 12-ounce glass with a couple tablespoons of ice cream of your preference and a splash of plain soda water. Mix very well with a spoon or put it in the blender and hit the "pulse" button a couple of times. Return to the glass, add a couple of more tablespoons ice cream (oh, what the heck, go for it—a scoop), top with soda to fill the glass, mix slightly. Top with whipped cream and a cherry and enjoy.

STRAWBERRY, PEACH, CHERRY, PINEAPPLE ICE CREAM SODAS

Prepare as above for plain ice cream soda, but add 1/4 cup of pureed fruit of choice to the milk and mix before adding the first bit of ice cream (flavor of your choice).

COOLERS AND FRUIT DRINKS

For the cooler and fruit drink aficionados.

During warm weather, there is nothing quite as quenching to our thirsts as a cooler or some sort of fruit drink. The trick to making a "successful" beverage like these is always to use very chilled fruit and other ingredient—such as ginger ale, soda, and juices. If you find that your drink is a bit too sweet, add a touch of lime or lemon juice. When using juice, use fresh juices whenever possible. When it comes to garnish for these types of drinks, the sky is almost the limit, considering that you can use almost every sort of fruit – cherries, lemon wedges, pineapple, kiwi and oranges, to name a few.

WINE COOLER

Might as well start off with an alcoholic cooler, for those who care to imbibe. Fill a 12-ounce glass with ice; add 1/2 glass of dry white or red wine, and fill the glass with club soda or ginger ale and stir. Top with a twist or wedge of lemon.

SANGRIA

This is a wonderful cooling drink to accompany a summer brunch. Fill a tall 12-ounce glass with ice, and 1 cup of a dry red wine, a splash of orange juice, and the peeled, curly rind of a lemon. Fill remainder of glass with club soda. Top with a fresh strawberry.

FRUIT COOLER

Fill a 12-ounce glass with ice; add 1/2 glass of fruit juice of your choice (orange, cherry, pineapple, apple, lime, cranberry, etc.) Fill remainder of glass with club soda or ginger ale and stir. Top with garnish of choice.

LEMON, ORANGE OR LIMEADE

In a 12-ounce glass, add 1/2 cup fresh fruit juice, sugar to sweeten as needed and fill with cold water. Stir and enjoy. Consider adding a splash of cranberry juice for additional flavor and color.

PUNCHES

When having a party it's often easier and less expensive to prepare a punch—alcoholic or otherwise. Guests can serve themselves, allowing the hosts to enjoy the party. There are endless creations in the "World of Punch;" we shall list some for your consideration.

All quantities are for 12 people (you can adjust quantities as needed):

ORANGE-LEMON PUNCH

Place a block of ice in a punch bowl. Mix 1 1/2 quarts of orange juice with 1 1/2 cups of lemon juice and 1/2 cup of Maraschino cherries and their syrup; pour over the ice. Pour 1 quart each of ginger ale and club soda into the punch. Gently stir prior to serving.

CRANBERRY-PINEAPPLE PUNCH

Place a block of ice in a punch bowl. Mix 1 1/2 quarts of pineapple juice with 1 1/2 cups cranberry juice and 2 cups crushed pineapple; pour over the ice block. Pour 1 quart each of ginger ale and club soda into the punch. Gently stir prior to serving.

HOT CIDER PUNCH

Combine 3 quarts apple cider with 1 pound dark brown sugar; pour into a large pot. Add 6 sticks of cinnamon, 12 whole cloves and a teaspoon of nutmeg, and simmer uncovered for 15 to 20 minutes. Strain into a large silver punch bowl, which will retain the heat. Float a dozen slices or wheels of lemon on top and serve.

CHAMPAGNE PUNCH

Blend together 2/3 cup lemon juice and 1/2 cup very fine granulated sugar in a large pot over low heat until sugar dissolves. Immediately remove from heat and set aside to cool. Mix in 2 cups cranberry juice with 1 cup brandy, and pour over a block of ice in punch bowl. Lastly, pour in 3 bottles champagne and 1 quart of club soda; gently mix. Float a dozen orange slices on top and serve.

RUM-EGGNOG PUNCH

Blend together 2 quarts of pre-made eggnog with a fifth of rum of your choice. Whip 1 pint heavy whipping cream until it peaks; then fold the cream into the nog and refrigerate in a punch bowl for at least an hour. Dust with cinnamon and nutmeg before serving.

WINE PUNCH

Place a block of ice in a punch bowl. Blend together 2 25-ounce bottles dry white wine and 3 quarts club soda with 1/4 cup fine granulated sugar and 1 quart light rum; pour over the ice. Float orange slices on top.

WINES

When it comes to wines, the subject could not be covered adequately, other than in volumes. In lieu of this, what we'd like to do is give you a general overview and prompt those interested to seek further knowledge from experts in the field. There are many fine books available which would enable you to gain considerable insight into the subject.

To the wine connoisseur, the old rules may still apply when deciding what wine goes with what food (red with red meat, and white with white meat), but today, that does not have to be taken as gospel truth. It is in great measure a matter of preference, tempered with a good bit of horse sense. Heavy wine with a delicate dish does seem out of place; equally out of place would be a delicate wine with a very hearty dish, but YOU are your own expert, so find what best works for your tastes.

DRY RED TABLE WINES

These dry red table wines are excellent served with meals.

American wine: Pinot Noir, Cabernet, Zinfandel and Gamay are really first rate -- quite excellent.

French Bordeaux: Wines such as St. Emilion, Château Mouton-Rothschild, Graves and Medoc should be considered full-bodied, rich and fragrant.

French Burgundy: Pommard and Beaujolais are classified as more robust and a bit heavier.

Rhone Valley wines: You'll find that wines from this region, such as Chateauneuf-du-Pape, are quite full-bodied.

Italian wines: The ever-popular Chianti, Bardolino, (smooth but similar to the Chianti) or the delicate Valpolicella go perfectly with Italian food.

Spanish wines: Among others, the robust Rioja is a nice accompaniment to any beef dish.

Portuguese wines: Among others, the Dao goes wonderfully with beef dishes also.

DRY WHITE TABLE WINES

American wines: Sauvignon Blanc, Chardonnay, Riesling and Chablis go well with delicate seafood dishes.

Portuguese wines: Look for the very tart Vinho Verde. It is best served very chilled and goes nicely with creamed pasta dishes.

Spanish wines: Look again for the Rioja label; it's nice served with rice dishes.

Italian wines: You'll find several good choices in this category. Look for the dry Orvieto, the light and smooth Soave, and the dry Verdicchio. Good served with seafood dishes.

German wines: This country produces a huge selection of quality wines. Look for the Rieslings, (note the Johannesburg, Germany's most famous); also, consider the Liebfraumilch (such as Blue Nun). These Rhine wines are generally fairly dry and light. In a Moselle wine, look for Piesporter.

French wines: The Graves is dry, along with the Poilly-Fume, and Vouvray. You'll find these wines are exceptional.

ROSE WINES
These wines are a bit sweeter and suitable to accompany white or red meats. All are well-known and wonderful.

American wines: Consider the Gamay and Grenache.

French wines: Look for Anjou.

Portuguese wines: A good choice is Mateus.

DESSERT WINES
These wines are sweet and heavier, which makes them especially nice when served with desserts. They include but are in no way limited to:

Sauternes: Consider the Chateau La Tour-Blanche.

Ports: Look for the mellow Tawny or the sweet Ruby. True "Portos" come from Porto, Portugal. These are exquisite; those from other places are just ordinary ports.

Madeiras: The dry Sercial and the sweet Malmsey are excellent choices.

Sherries: You'll enjoy the mellow and dry Manzanilla, the medium-dry Amontillado, and the sweet Cream Sherry, all of which trace their origins to Jerez, Spain.

Tokays: Either white or sweet, are made from the Tokay grape.

Muscatels: These extra-sweet wines come from Spain, Greece and Portugal.

SPARKLING WINES AND CHAMPAGNE

Champagnes come from the province of Champagne in France and are the only true champagnes; that product (a blend of white wine made from Pinot grapes) is the only one that can legally carry the name "Champagne" in Europe. In the United States, while we tend to think of it as "true" champagne, ours is merely a sparkling wine. We make many varieties which are excellent.

WINE TERMINOLOGY

It would be impossible to do justice to ALL the terms surrounding the wines of the world; however, we list a few of those you may come into contact with on a more frequent basis.

CLOS: This is the French term for vineyard (such as Clos de Bois).

APPELLATION CONTROLEE: The French guarantee of place of origin and high standards.

CAVE: The French word for wine cellar.

V.D.Q.S.: While this looks and sounds impressive, it simply means that the wine was produced under regulation of the government.

VIN BLANC: The French term for white wine.

VIN ROUGE: The French term for red wine.

VIN ORDINAIRE: The common French red or white table wines.

DRY: Wines that are not sweet.

SEC: Sweet.

BRUT: Dry.

VINTAGE: Refers to the year of the grape crop.

LIQUORS

This field is one that is so immense as to be mind-boggling. We opt to cover some of the basics, many of which may be well-known to you. In any case, the one point we want to stress when consuming ANY alcoholic product is MODERATION and common sense.

So that you can gain some knowledge to become the "Bartender du Jour" at your next party, let us give you a few hints; your guests will think you're a pro.

- A cocktail served "up" (like a martini) is served in a cocktail glass.
- A "pony" is a one-ounce bar measure.
- To "stir" is to mix, using a long-handled spoon in a circular motion.
- A "twist" isn't the dance; it's a twisted piece of lemon rind.
- To "shake" is to blend by shaking in a covered shaker.
- "On the rocks" is not a marriage in trouble; it's a drink over ice.
- "Neat" doesn't mean really cool; it's straight shots without ice.
- A "dash" when used at a bar means about 7 or 8 drops.

WHISKIES

Whiskies are all liquors themselves, and are distilled from grain mash such as corn, rye, wheat and barley.

Some examples include:

Rye: distilled from rye mash.

Irish: a dry whiskey distilled from grain.

Scotch: a blend of grain and malt whiskies.

Straight: aged rye or bourbon, unblended grain whiskey.

Blended: a light blend of neutral spirits and 100 proof straight whiskies.

Canadian: a smooth liquor distilled from blends of rye, corn, wheat and barley.

Corn: the infamous "moonshine" distilled from fermented corn mash.

LIQUORS

All liquors do not fall into the category of whiskies, and are distilled from various items, such as grains, cactus (for tequila), sugar cane (for rum) and potatoes (for vodka).

Some popular liquors include:

Vodka: distilled from potatoes (or fermented grain mash) and charcoal filtered.

Gin: dry neutral distilled grain with a touch of juniper.

Aquavit: this Scandinavian liquor is distilled from grain mash or potato with a touch of caraway. Very potent and usually drunk iced.

Bourbon: distilled from fermented mash of rye, corn and malt barley. Distinctly American, it is rich and very smooth. "Straight" bourbon must contain at least 51 percent corn mash. "Blended" bourbon, must contain at least 51 percent straight bourbon.

Southern Comfort: a bourbon mixed with peach liquor and aged for many months; sweet, powerful.

Rum: distilled from sugar cane, it ranges from very light to amber to full-bodied dark brown.

Tequila: distilled from fermented cactus; potent/100 proof.

COCKTAILS

There are literally hundreds of alcoholic beverages that are classics and very well known. Usually these cocktails are served prior to meals or at cocktail parties. As we have shown, wine is the choice with meals, and dessert wines or an after-dinner cordial go nicely after a meal. We shall list a few of the many before-meal or party choices in cocktails for you:

TOM COLLINS

Place 2 ounces of gin, 1 teaspoon sugar and 1 tablespoon of lemon juice in a tall 12-ounce glass and stir. Add ice and club soda and stir. Garnish with a cherry.

JOHN COLLINS

Same as Tom Collins, only substitute blended whiskey.

BLOODY MARY

This one is great anytime, but particularly during breakfasts or brunches. In a tall 12-ounce glass, add ice, 2 ounces of vodka, a splash of Worcestershire sauce, 1/2 teaspoon horseradish, a dash of celery seed, a splash of Tabasco, and tomato juice. Stir briskly with a long-handled spoon. Garnish with the traditional stalk of celery or a pickled pole bean. *Get ready for spicy!*

RUSTY NAIL

Add ice to an 8-ounce rocks glass; pour 1 1/4 ounces Scotch and 3/4 ounce Drambuie over the rocks. Stir and serve.

WHISKEY SOUR

In a cocktail shaker, combine crushed ice with 1 1/4 ounces of whiskey and 3 ounces bar mix; shake and strain into a cocktail glass. You can also shake without ice and serve over ice in an 8-ounce rocks glass. Garnish with a cherry.

MARTINI

In a bar mixing glass, add ice with 2 1/2 ounces of either gin or vodka, and 1/2 ounce dry vermouth (for what is known as a "wet" martini) or just a breath of vermouth for the more preferable very dry martini. Stir and strain into a cocktail glass or pour over ice into a rocks glass. Garnish with an olive or twist of lemon.

MANHATTAN

In a bar mixing glass, add ice with 2 1/2 ounces of whiskey, and 1/2 ounce sweet vermouth. (For a "Dry Manhattan", use dry vermouth). Stir and strain into a cocktail glass or pour over ice into a rocks glass. Garnish with a cherry or twist of lemon. *For what is known as a "Perfect Manhattan," use equal parts of sweet and dry vermouth.*

LONG ISLAND ICED TEA
No, you're not seeing things! This is not your grandmother's iced tea. This one will sneak up on you and, before you know it, you'll be VERY happy! Add ice to a tall 12-ounce glass; pour 1/4 ounce EACH of vodka, gin, tequila, light rum and triple sec over the ice; fill remainder of glass with lemon bar mix. Pour mixture into shaker; shake and return to the glass. Top with a splash of Coke and serve. *Hold onto your seat!*

PINK LADY
Your girlfriend or mom will love this one! Mix 3/4 ounce of gin, 3/4 ounce white crème de cacao, a splash of grenadine and 3 ounces cream in a shaker. Shake and strain into a cocktail glass.

BLACK RUSSIAN
Pour 1 1/4 ounces of vodka and 3/4 ounce of kahlua over ice in an 8-ounce rock glass.

CHAMPAGNE COCKTAIL
Pour champagne into a champagne glass over a cube of sugar with a dash of bitters.

MARGARITA
Wet the rim of a 4 1/2ounce cocktail glass with lime juice and then dip the rim in salt to frost the rim. Add 1 1/4 ounces tequila, 3/4 ounce triple sec, a splash of lime juice and 2 1/4 ounces lemon bar mix in a shaker. Shake and strain into the glass. Garnish with a wedge of lime.

SCREWDRIVER
Fill a 12-ounce glass with ice, add 1 1/4 ounces vodka and fill with orange juice. Garnish with an orange slice. *Nice at brunches.*

SALTY DOG
Salt the rim of a tall 12-ounce glass. Add ice and pour 1 1/4 ounces of vodka and fill with grapefruit juice. A similar drink—a GREYHOUND—is the same, except no salt on the glass rim.

MIMOSA
Mix three parts champagne and one part chilled orange juice in a champagne glass, or over ice in a tall 12-ounce glass if preferred. *Another great brunch drink.*

HARVEY WALLBANGER
This is really a Screwdriver, BUT with the addition of a hearty lacing of Galliano.

FUZZY NAVEL

In a 12-ounce glass, add 1 1/4 ounces peach schnapps and fill with orange juice. For a HAIRY NAVEL, prepare with 3/4 ounce each of vodka and schnapps.

CUBA LIBRA

This one is a nice midday cooler. In a 12-ounce glass, add ice and 1 1/4 ounces rum. Fill glass with Coke and ALWAYS garnish with a lime wedge.

AFTER-DINNER COCKTAILS AND CORDIALS

BRANDY ALEXANDER

Add ice and 1 1/4 ounces brandy, 3/4 ounce crème de cacao, and 3 ounces cream in a shaker. Shake and strain into a cocktail glass.

GRASSHOPPER

Add 3/4 ounce green crème de menthe, 3/4 ounce white crème de cacao and 3 ounces cream in a shaker. Shake and strain into a cocktail glass.

IRISH COFFEE

Add 1 1/2 ounces Irish whiskey to a coffee mug; fill with hot coffee. Top with whipped cream and a drizzle of green crème de menthe. *This a great cold weather drink sipped by a roaring fire.*

STINGER

Pour 1 1/4 ounces brandy or cognac and 3/4 ounce white crème de menthe over ice in an 8-ounce rock glass.

LIQUEURS

There are a plethora of these, and we obviously shall not cover them all here; suffice it to note that they are usually served as an after-meal cordial drink, with or without ice:

Anisette: an aromatic (anise) sweet liqueur.

Apricot: a fragrant, syrupy liqueur from apricots.

Armagnac: a dry French brandy.

Benedictine: a secret recipe, originating with French monks. Very sweet and fruity.

B&B: a 50 percent mix each of Benedictine and brandy.

Brandy: technically either a fermented juice or distilled wine product, which is aged in wood.

Cognac: a choice brandy, made in France.

Calvados: a fine apple brandy of France.

Chartreuse: a pale-green or gold colored, brandy-based liqueur; originated with the monks of France.

Cherry Heering: a cherry-flavored liqueur from Denmark.

Cointreau: an orange-flavored French liqueur.

Drambuie: a pale Scotch-based liqueur.

Galliano: a gold Italian liqueur.

Grand Marnier: an orange-flavored, cognac-based liqueur from France.

Kahlua: a Mexican liqueur, made from cocoa bean and coffee.

Metaxa: a heavy and sweet brandy from Greece.

Ouzo: a licorice Greek brandy, usually mixed with water.

Pernod: a yellow licorice liqueur, mixed with water.

Strega: a very flowery Italian liqueur.

Tia Maria: a coffee, rum-based liqueur.

Triple Sec: an orange-flavored liqueur, similar to Curacao.

BEERS

When most people think of beer, they consider all malt beverages as beers. In actuality, there are beers AND ales. The difference in these beverages is that beers are a light, bubbly brew, while ales are much heavier.

American tastes prefer a chilled brew, while the ideal is about 40 degrees. The choice is yours.

Acknowledgements

In gratitude for sharing their recipes, vast amounts of information about foods and their preparation, and their encouragement and expertise, without which this book would not have been realized:

Jay Bithoney

Emily Bithoney Kozzi

Jill Brown, general manager, Rancho Mirage MHC, Rancho Mirage, Calif.

Paul Cavaliere, owner, Colony House Catering, Summit Point, W. Va.

Theresa Fontaine

Fias Co. Farms

Tim Glasby

Jo-Ann Killion-Pedigo

The Left Bank Restaurants, Palm Springs and Rancho Mirage, Calif.

New England Inn, Intervale, N.H.

Pomme Frite Restaurant, Boston, Mass.

Rodney Long

Bob Peterson

Kate Porter

Helen Robinson

Lillian Robinson

Kate Sisson

Fred Tamucci

Fabio Travasini

Sam Wertz

Pam Winslow

Marcelle Wilson

Thanks also to:

American Academy of Clinical Nutrition

American Heart Association

American Lamb Council

American Medical Association

Food and Nutrition Board

National Academy of Sciences

National Dairy Council

National Pasta Association

National Research Council

Palm Springs Public Library

United States Department of Agriculture

MORE COMMON SENSE FROM GRANDMA

(While these are not "cooking" hints, this is good stuff you ought to know!)

- Got a headache? Cut a lime in half and rub it on your forehead. The throbbing should cease.

- Another "sure-cure" for a headache? Drink two large glasses of warm water.

- Can't open that jar? Put on a latex dishwashing glove. It'll give you a non-slip surface and presto, the jar is open.

- Got a mosquito bite? Itching like crazy? Put plain old soap on the offending area and get instant relief.

- Use air freshener to clean the mirrors; does a super job and smells nice too.

- Got a splinter? Before you reach for the needle or tweezers, get out the Scotch tape or duct tape, put a piece over the splinter, and pull it out.

- Clean up as you go: It's much easier than facing a mountain of pots, pans, dishes and bowls later.

- If there's a question for which you have no answer, don't be afraid to ask someone.

You thought Alka-Seltzer was only for a hangover or upset stomach? Nay, Nay, Nay. Read on:

- To clean a toilet, drop in two tablets, wait 20 minutes, brush and flush.

- To clean a vase, fill with water, drop in two tablets (same for stained coffee cups)

- To clean jewelry, drop two tablets in a glass of water, immerse the jewelry. Wait two minutes, rinse and dry.

- To clean a thermos, fill with water and drop in four tablets. Let soak for an hour, then rinse.

- To unclog a drain, drop three tablets down the drain, followed by a cup of white vinegar. Wait two or three minutes and flush with hot water.

TEST ANSWERS FROM PAGE 30

1. Yes. Humans need 3 to 8 grams of salt daily.

2. No one salt is less harmful than another; salt is salt.

3. Two salt alternatives: you can use mint, lemon, dill, pepper, onion, ginger, wine, cinnamon, basil, chives, paprika, parsley, green pepper, bay leaf, thyme, mustard, curry, garlic, tomato or oregano.

4. False. Sodium nitrate is a preservative used in prepared meats.

5. False. The government can't watch everything you ingest; many additives are questionable or just not healthy.

6. An average 30-year-old male needs 56 grams of protein daily.

7. False. Vitamin A requirements vary from 2,000 to 5,000 IU daily.

8. False. Mg. stands for milligram.

9. True. Fresh carrots contain a very high concentration of Vitamin A —15,230 IU per cup.

10. False. Asparagus contains very little sodium – about 1 milligram per cup. Turnips and spinach are among vegetables with the highest concentration of sodium.

11. True. Mangos are a terrific source of Vitamin A

12. A cup of whole milk contains about 159 calories.

13. Teflon-coated cookware is tops overall.

14. Blanch means "to briefly immerse in boiling water."

15. False. Al dente is an Italian term meaning "tender but firm."

16. One fluid ounce is equal to about 2 tablespoons.

17. A moderate oven is about 350 degrees.

18. A pound of raisins is equal to about three cups.

19. Herbs are leaves of temperate, fragrant biennials and annuals; Spices are roots, stems, fruits and leaves of more tropical perennials.

20. Ginger is often used in Asian cooking.

NOTES:

NOTES:

"Remember, some things have to be
believed to be seen."
—Ralph Hodgson

NOTES:

NOTES:

Order a title from the ABCs of Business series!

A Public Relations Survival Kit
by S. E. Slack   ISBN 0-9714988-0-6 $24.95   176 pp.

Discover the truth about public relations - that it's easy, it's logical and it doesn't have to cost half your budget. Slack takes on the myth that smaller businesses can't handle public relations without help and delivers this knock-out punch: Public relations is not rocket science. PR consultants just want you to think it is.

GRENDEL
PRESS

Order from your local bookstore or by visiting the Grendel Press Web site at **http://www.grendelpress.com** Or take advantage of the special offer below!

SPECIAL MAIL ORDER OFFER: 25% OFF WITH THIS FORM

NAME: _____

ADDRESS: _____

CITY, ST & ZIP: _____

PHONE: _____

Quantity: _____ @ **$18.71** = _____

3.7% Tax: _____
(CO residents only)

S&H: $4.95 _____
(add $1.35 for each addt'l book)

Total: $ _____

☐ **MY CHECK IS ENCLOSED**
☐ **VISA** ☐ **M/C** ☐ **DISCOVER**
(All areas of this form MUST be completed to process credit card)

Card #: _____

Expiration date: _____

Name as it appears on card:

_____

MAIL TO: **Grendel Press
ATTN: Special Orders Dept.
Offer: PRKIT200202
P.O. Box 238
Loveland, CO 80539-0238**

Thank You!